## Stanley Spei.....

Jane Draycott's collections include *The Occupant* (Carcanet, a PBS 2016 Recommendation), *Over* (TS Eliot Prize shortlist 2009), and *Prince Rupert's Drop* (Forward Poetry Prize shortlist 1999). Her translation of the medieval elegy *Pearl* (2011) was a *Times* Stephen Spender Prize-winner. Work from her Two Rivers Press collection *Tideway* (2002, illustrations by Peter Hay) was nominated for the Forward Prize for Best Single Poem.

Carolyn Leder is a recognized scholar on Stanley Spencer, a long-standing Trustee of the Stanley Spencer Gallery, and Consultant to three volumes of Spencer writings, edited by John Spencer 2016–18. She is in *Who's Who in Art*, and is regularly consulted on Spencer by Sotheby's. Her publications include a book on Spencer's Scrapbook drawings and numerous exhibition catalogues.

Peter Robinson has published aphorisms, short stories, various works of literary criticism and a novel, and has been awarded the Cheltenham Prize, the John Florio Prize and two PBS Recommendations for some of his books of poetry and translation. He is Professor of English and American Literature at the University of Reading and poetry editor for Two Rivers Press.

# Cookham Festival Stanley Spencer Poetry Competition

### Don and Jill Cawthorne Prize

The major prize in the 2017 Cookham Festival Stanley Spencer Poetry Competition is awarded in memory of Don and Jill Cawthorne, who made Cookham their home and who worked tirelessly to the benefit of the local community. They supported the Festival over many years and embodied the spirit of 'Growing the Arts'.

Don and Jill died within two days of each other in May 2016, after more than fifty years of marriage.

### Other awards

The Stationers' Company Award is sponsored by the Worshipful Company of Stationers and Newspaper Makers.

The Maidenhead Advertiser Award is supported by Baylis Media Ltd, publishers of the *Maidenhead Advertiser*.

# Stanley Spencer Poems

## An Anthology

First published in the UK in 2017 by Two Rivers Press
7 Denmark Road, Reading RG1 5PA.
www.tworiverspress.com

ISBN 978-1-909747-27-2

1 2 3 4 5 6 7 8 9

Two Rivers Press is represented in the UK by Inpress Ltd
and distributed by NBNi.

Cover design by Nadja Guggi using *The Neighbours*, 1936 (oil on canvas),
Spencer, Stanley (1891–1959). © Stanley Spencer Gallery, Cookham,
Berkshire, UK/Bridgeman Images
Text design by Nadja Guggi and typeset in Pollen and Parisine

Printed and bound in Great Britain by Conservatree

## Acknowledgements

On behalf of the Cookham Festival 2017, we wish to acknowledge with great thanks the help and support we have received from many sources in organizing what has been a memorable poetry competition. Particular thanks must go to Professor Peter Robinson of the University of Reading, whose idea the competition was in the first place, and to his fellow judges, the poet Jane Draycott and the noted art historian and Stanley Spencer Gallery Trustee Carolyn Leder. The competition could not have taken place without the support and sponsorship of the Trustees of the Estate of Don and Jill Cawthorne, the Worshipful Company of Stationers and Newspaper Makers and the *Maidenhead Advertiser*. The help and guidance of Sally Mortimore and her team at Two Rivers Press were essential in the assembly and production of the anthology of the seventy-eight longlisted entries, which will provide an enduring memento of the competition. Sir Stanley Spencer's grandson, John Spencer, kindly helped us with issues of copyright and the volunteers and trustees of the Stanley Spencer Gallery in Cookham provided invaluable advice and generously donated use of the Gallery for the competition launch and awards ceremony.

We also need to thank some two hundred poets, both from the UK and overseas, who responded so magnificently to the challenge, and last, but by no means least, the members of the volunteer team at the Cookham Festival who put in many hours of their time organizing the competition.

*The Cookham Festival Team 2017*

# Contents

# Introduction

Stanley Spencer (1891–1959) was undoubtedly one of the most admired and influential English painters of the twentieth century. The Thames valley village of Cookham, just to the north of Maidenhead, was a major influence on both his life and painting. His reference to the place as 'a village in Heaven' is exemplified in the many paintings dramatizing Biblical scenes that he set there, featuring recognizable local people. Contributing to the fiftieth anniversary of the Cookham Festival, the anthology you are holding in your hands is a long-list selection from the more than two hundred and fifty entries to the 2017 Stanley Spencer Poetry Competition, which invited poets to find inspiration for their own art in the work of this remarkable man. The poet Jane Draycott, art historian and Spencer expert Carolyn Leder, and I selected these poems, from which we then made the shortlist of specially commended entries, which, in turn, after much fascinating and enlightening discussion, produced the three prize-winning poems.

Though the word was not used in the notice announcing the competition, among the invited submissions we imagined were 'ekphrastic poems'. 'Ekphrastic', deriving from 'ekphrasis' – Greek for 'description', is now regularly used to characterize poems, and there are a great many of them that take their inspiration from another work of art, most usually a painting, and that base their insights upon a description of the chosen artwork. We were not disappointed, and a number of the poems in this anthology borrow for their titles the names given to Spencer's own paintings, ones such as 'Hilda, Unity and Dolls, 1937', 'Zacharias and Elizabeth, 1914', 'Double Nude Portrait, 1937', and 'Port Glasgow Cemetery, 1947'. The great justification for these kinds of poems must be this: since the works that inspire them are eloquently silent, in their giving voice to a painting's appearance and significance, they can draw out more explicitly its themes and implications. Yet, at the same time, they will need to avoid the appearance of versified art criticism, by using the techniques of their own generic form to achieve art status themselves. Reading this anthology is to encounter a series of object lessons in how such a balance among the challenges of description, commentary, and poem can be achieved.

With *Christ Preaching at Cookham Regatta*, 1958   Credit: John Neal

Spencer's own interest in poetry, especially work with a religious theme, can be sensed from his 1911 painting *John Donne Arriving in Heaven*, where the seventeenth-century poet and Dean of St Paul's is imagined as walking across Widbrook Common near Cookham. Inspired by a reading of Donne's Sermon 64, the picture finds the posthumous writer and divine encountering a number of saintly figures praying in different directions, all of which directions are thoroughly English in character. It is as if Spencer's answer would have been an emphatic *Yes* to William Blake's question at the opening of his poem usually called 'Jerusalem' as to whether the feet of Jesus did 'Walk upon England's mountains green?'

Writing from RAMC, 143rd Field Ambulance, Salonika, on 17 July 1917, Spencer confided that 'I am reading Keats & Blake at the same time. Can anything be more scathing than Blake's epigrams on the artists of his time? I wish he had been alive today'. Then he asks whether 'you think Blake's lyrics such as "my silks and fine array" & "How sweet I roamed from field to field" are comparable with Shakespeare's?' Then he reports his evaluation of these two great Romantic poets:

> I love Keats more than Blake, but I think Blake is an infinitely greater man than Keats. Blake is free. Everything comes from Blake, with apparently no effort, clear and pure as the light of God. But Keats is only at times inspired. As Jacques Raverat said of me, so I say of Keats: he 'interfered with the Holy Ghost'. Blake had perfect faith, which accounts for the ease one feels in reading Blake. There is not this ease with Keats ... Keats was a perfectly good man, but he did not realise the importance of knowing always the time of his visitation. His faith was shaky & that is why I do not feel as happy when I read Keats as I do when I read Blake. But I cannot read Blake for long. He is like Bach – rather overpowering. I have been living with that most gracious & benign comforter. John Milton.

Elsewhere in this correspondence from his overseas posting Spencer notes that he has books by Chaucer and Shakespeare, and he alludes to William Cowper's hymn 'On Africa's Coral Shore'.

In Holy Trinity Churchyard, Cookham, 1950s

In High Road, Cookham Rise, 1950s

With the famous pram, 1950s

This anthology's seventy-eight poems by sixty-three poets presented here find inspiration in a great range of the painter's experiences and works. Though Cookham predominates, and a number of the writers evidently visiting the Stanley Spencer Gallery before composing their entries, inspiration has been drawn from a great many aspects of the artist's life and work. While his relations with the village where he spent most of his time would appear idyllic, those between the figures in his private experience of relationship look from their representations in his work as less so – his sometimes torturous involvements with the women in his life, whom he repeatedly portrayed in paintings and drawings, figuring frequently in poems gathered here. Yet these poems are often simply responding to the evidence of such challenging double portrait paintings as those showing the artist with his second wife, Patricia Preece, both of them naked. His first, Hilda, and his children, also feature – as do the complexities of his emotional life and the intensely scrutinizing, near-confessional self-portraits that he painted throughout. Spencer's ability to make art from the detail and circumstance of his life will also likely have endeared him to poets.

Painting *The Crucifixion* in 1957   Credit: John Neal

So too his contributions to the country's social history of war and industry figure in poems anthologized here – ones that conjure up the Port Glasgow shipyard paintings made during the Second World War, as well as his own Great War experiences in uniform at the Beaufort War Hospital, Fishponds, Bristol, and during his posting overseas that took him to Salonika and Karasuli in Macedonia. His experiences in Bristol and the Balkans are prominently represented in the wall paintings he made for The Sandham Memorial Chapel, 1927–1932, at Burghclere, another place that it isn't difficult to imagine some of the poets anthologized here visiting before they set pen to paper.

Spencer's 1937 painting *Southwold*, on display at the Cookham Gallery during the period of the competition, and also picked out for poetry here, intriguingly and evocatively illustrates his feeling for places viewed from unusual angles. The poets anthologized have also admired and responded to the painter's ability to paint the most mundane of things. He had the gift of making them come alive, especially under a steady and diffused English light. Even when not particularly indicated, as it is in the paintings of symbolic or Biblical themes, his pictures interweave the spiritual with the everyday, and especially so in ones which catch the detail of street scenes and back yards, or boat yards in Cookham for instance, ones painted with a sharply focused accuracy, which manage to be infused with his spiritual vision while not underlining it in his signature distortions and fondly caricatured figure drawing. Indeed, at the heart of Spencer's gift is the ability to render anything and everything, however nondescript, as having meaning in its own right. That, perhaps, is the poet in him – and another reason why the poets anthologized responded so warmly to his art.

Uppermost among his works, of course, are his representations of life in the Thames Valley. The writer and poet Helen MacDonald took *Swan Upping at Cookham*, for instance, as a starting point in her *New York Times Magazine* article dated 5 January 2017 and entitled 'In Search of Post-Brexit England'. In this piece, concerned with what it 'means to call a country home', she points out that the painting was left 'half-finished in his bedroom in Cookham when he went off to war in 1915, and the knowledge that it was there sustained him over the next three years.' MacDonald draws attention to what is involved in the ancient practice of swan upping, noting that the 'crews check the parentage of young birds and place a mark on them to claim their ownership: Some belong to the queen, others to the Worshipful Company of Vintners and the Worshipful Company of Dyers, two ancient trade guilds based in the City of London.' In drawing upon Spencer's painting, she not only raises questions about projective possession of the country, its flora and fauna, and who has responsibility for its well-being, but also pays further tribute to what she calls 'the mystical, eccentric English artist Stanley Spencer'.

Surviving unfinished paintings reveal how this artist would paint across an underdrawn and squared up canvas, filling it in with paint, bit by bit, until complete. This working process may also show in *Swan Upping at Cookham,* interrupted, as MacDonald notes, while Spencer served his country in the Great War. For it is as if the Thames river water, with its characteristically emblematic wave forms, hinges under t bridge, where the mood and mode of the painting migh registering the shock of that interruption and chang so, Spencer's paintings, that are themselves a baror English life and history in the near sixty years of his have inspired very different styles of poem – ar

xviii

Painting *Helter Skelter, Hampstead Heath* 1937
Credit: J.B. Rustomjee

mixing works deeply founded in the craft and technique of English lyric poetry with experiments in the collaging of his words, and styles that began to emerge in the early years of his century, which he will have first encountered at the Slade. We can also see from photographs of Spencer at work how public a way of making art his could be, with children and local people taking a look and perhaps commenting on what he as an artist would do all day.

Being involved with this project, and reading through the entries we received, as well as discussing them with Jane and Carolyn at the Henley Rowing Museum in December 2016, would have an unexpected impact on my own inspiration when, only a day or so later, I was taken by Professor Adam Piette to visit the Graves Art Gallery in Sheffield and found myself face to face with Stanley Spencer's *Helter Skelter, Hampstead Heath* – a painting from which none of the poems entered had happened to take inspiration. So perhaps I can be permitted to end these brief introductory comments for *Stanley Spencer Poems: An Anthology* by offering my own poem, 'What's Left', with its passing tribute to this genius of 'some stubborn British art', Stanley Spencer's, unexpectedly discovered in the same gallery as a painting set on the European continent by David Bomberg, one of his contemporaries at the Slade:

# What's Left

*for Adam Piette*

Starting from the earliest
terrace on this hillside,
it's all downhill from here
and reassuring, solid
house-fronts line the way
to a scheduled train by way
of some stubborn British art –
like Spencer's *Helter Skelter*
or a Bomberg Spanish landscape,
for instance, with this strange,
estranging afterlife
on wooded, green expanses
and Parkhill frieze of flats;
they're holding steadfast, steady,
as if composed before me
like a swansong for what's left.

*Peter Robinson*

## Note from the publisher

We have published these poems as submitted with very few, very minor grammatical amendments. We have standardized the format of the attributions but not changed the content, not even to correct titles or dates.

We are grateful to The Stanley Spencer Gallery Photographic Archive for permission to reproduce the photographs in the Introduction.

The words in Shez Courtenay-Smith's poem 'Deletions, Dear Desmond (August 1916)' are entirely those of Stanley Spencer, distilled with the use of 'deletions only' from Spencer's letter of August 1916 (held at the Stanley Spencer Gallery, Cookham) to his friend Desmond Chute. The distillation reproduced here is with kind permission of John Spencer and the Spencer Estate. Idiosyncratic spellings are Spencer's own.

Very sadly, Helen Kidd died just before this book went to press. She was a leading light in Oxford's poetry community, where her loss is deeply felt. For thirty years she was a generous and inspiring teacher of creative writing at Ruskin College, Oxford Brookes University, and lately with the Department of Continuing Education at the University of Oxford. She took over from Tom Rawling to convene an influential poetry workshop at the Old Fire Station for several years, and more recently joined in workshops with Back Room Poets. She also brought poetry to schools, care homes, hospices and other institutions across the county, sometimes in collaboration with her musician friends Isabel Knowland and Arne Richards. She was editor of three poetry magazines and her own work appeared in two pamphlets and three collections, details of which are in her biography at the end of the book.

# Darko's Ode:
# everything's stone so I say stay low

meanwhile    somewhere    Saussure invents
the cyanometer measuring    the fervid blueness    of the sky

I'll wrap    my arms    around

& for malingerers/like me/everything's    stone    so I say
stay low/pinch deep earth at pit & fire look to shale to sediment
metamorphically transformed to mica    in afterglow look

to exocarpic fossil shaft    & cleft's chastity/ erasure/ pre-history's
interstices    meanwhile my Tulip Poplars    despite themselves
root on rock fruiting paper-winged embryonic    samaras
whirlybirds    far as I'm    concerned volunteer
persistently/upright wherever they

wrap your    arms    around around

& in the rayless spark of these aphotic    eyes
of indefatigable/ of remonstrance    the past modeling the present &/or
the future    it's said we all fall to the side    we favor &
it's said around here rock    is human    prescribed
to our purposes    split carve cut    & arc    a sacred
dog    an original name for    horse    packs & pulls but those people

are mostly    gone & so I sow my seeds by moonlight    for double
blossom heads &    coyotes' ranks & regiments sleep
in rows muzzles on paws    awakening
at my approach one's up on her haunches stares down
the barrel    of a shotgun the others follow/ surround/ protect me

assisted evolution?    I wonder about that    about    who's doing

the caring & chemically rebuilding dying coral reefs    huh
meanwhile my chandeliers/ barn finds/ mended crystalline
shivers tinkles clinks    the cause of that shudder the rumble
of the nearby quarry mine    reminds me of

Darko sweet boy died      & loved      thigh high patent leather boots
& gleaming sculpted porcelain lips & other boys he thought
covened stroked just another one of nature's another      one of ours

I'll wrap      my arms      around

I need a word      for lovingly changed or
reshaped & I can't      find it he thought he      could be finessed
or flat-out      altered & I wonder how things fold in
on themselves finally disappearing      chinks piles of

discarded bones oyster shells cheap chipped china heaps
of accidents anchored or anchorless keep me in one piece
in one place      emboweled & buried howl & hot pressed
trapped/melting magma caving languorously in the breath

of our own      extravagant elegant      weight
wrap your      arms      around      around

& everything      shining and shimmering so bright it's nearly
an embarrassment & countries' hostages held in cabinets
stir & jostle      classifications/ curiosities      one mystery
to the page & our very own continents where we live      our time

a whirl a fly & eat & drink up & piney reach exceeding we hardly knew
what we meant/nations of atoms named      & set to work
enveloped as oxygen carbon hydrogen nitrogen calcium
phosphorescence/buckling glows of want/confederacies

of heavens & marshes & moraines &      oh      OH      we wonders
of the careful unfamiliar oh      we empires of blood      belonging

*MARA ADAMATIZ SCRUPE*

# Swan-Upper

First thing I return to the river
where last night, as swans retook possession,
you tied your skiff *Rosalind*
alongside the other five outside The Ferry
and using those boats as stepping stones –
a man who works on water would –
you came to me.

Yours is the Tideway with its chronicle
of springs and neaps, its ebb and flood
and clinging fog; you sense the moon exact her pull,
taste the salt on an east wind
but now you've pulled ashore in our quiet reach,
a two day row from Staines
for the Vintners, Dyers and Royal swan-uppers:

boat builders, tug boat drivers, a rowing coach
and David, the Queen's swan marker –
white quill poking from his hat –
trailed by an entourage of vintage boats
with their perfect paintwork and ice-buckets
out for a week long booze-up
while you catch and count swans.

No-one about this early,
but last night, you – Thames waterman,
Master of the Woolwich ferry –
in your red t-shirt and white trousers half mast
with sockless ankles and pumps with no laces,
your dark curls wilting,
how good it felt.

*VIRGINA ASTLEY*

# The Last Willow Pot Omper Maker

Yesterday, by the main road, was a large man –
purple plastic basket at the foot of his ladder
He started on the low branches, then
like a waxwing stripping a rowan,
worked his way through the tree.

His basket wasn't enough,
apples piled at his feet
and I thought of the old man in Evesham,
with his orchard and its purple Pershore plums,
and the willow pots he wove to carry this fruit,

of the two-up, two-down, the fourteen children
each with their own job:
gloves sewn, sprouts picked, pigs raised
how he'd lived there all his life, he'd said
*Crows are just as black across the vale.*

*VIRGINIA ASTLEY*

# Moulsford to Cleeve

Hemp agrimony, angelica, willowherb
insist their names are read aloud –
a towpath recitative

half-said, half-sung, as the river sleeps,
curls into a backwater
on the longest reach without a lock

where there were always dairy cows,
turgid udders swaying
as they grazed their way across

the meadows, and you must remember
those sultry afternoons
how they'd wade in

and with legs half-immersed
lower their heads to drink,
flies still mithering;

those fields beyond too,
how they blazed that time
the wind bellowed the stubble fire

and hearing a siren score the night air
we opened the door to watch
flames taking hold,
                           blow-torching the hill.

*VIRGINA ASTLEY*

# Don't those background figures look like cricketers?

*'Unveiling a War Memorial at Cookham', 1921, by Stanley Spencer*

They aren't here, admiring the memorial.
They're years away in that July when war stopped play –
whole summers lost with all the runs they might have scored
but for the need to push a dead bat down the pitch
to smother spin or, on the back foot, fend off bouncers
delivered from the old Pavilion End at Ypres.

Some stand apart like batsmen in that no man's land
of waiting to go in. They know they'll be redundant
once they're out and end up getting sent to guard
the boundary on solitary sentry-go.
No one volunteers to be the deep third man
who's picked off by a sniper crouched in Plugstreet Wood.

The monument's a scoreboard, listing those who've been
dismissed – but with no indication of 'how out'.
Reclining figures look asleep but could be corpses
laid out in white flannels and new county caps,
awarded in the bodyline of duty when
the tail held on to force a draw at Passchendaele.

A timeless cricket tea awaits them: infinite
white table cloths and maids in mob caps serving scones
with pots of strawberry preserve – not lethal tins
of trench-grade plum & apple mixed by Tickler girls.
The clubhouse clock hands can't get past the moment when
the sun first slipped behind the sightscreen on the Somme.

*MICHAEL BARTHOLOMEW-BIGGS*

During the First World War Ticklers won a government contract
to supply front lines with plum-and-apple jam. It was said to come
"in two colours, green and red both tasting the same". Empty jam tins
were allegedly used as makeshift grenades

# Shrines

*After 'Washing Lockers' by Stanley Spencer*

Kneeling here in the bathroom,
wedged between two magenta tubs –
pinned into sackcloth apron,
I could almost be saying a prayer
while the other orderlies follow the call
of carbolic, scour hospital lockers –
wash away the stains of war.
Here in this sacred space
I'm taking time out from the wounded,
those avenues of iron bedsteads,
red and white blossom of flesh.

I find comfort in cleanliness,
the brisk rub of soap on wood grain so different
from gentle dabs of swabs on skin.
These temples are temporary homes
for Tommy's treatures: The water jug,
drinking cup. Stuff from home:
photos, letters, fags, stubs of pencils,
the daywear *hospital blues* neatly folded;
something to do in quiet times,
a book, a paper, perhaps a pack of cards
for playing patience.

As I kneel here quietly in ward four
I think of the men patched up,
sent back, as we scrub their
life-prints away, their personal effects
pocketed in uniforms again – small things
carried into battle, returned to families,
relics of war re-housed in other shrines now:
side-boards, cupboards, bedside tables –
and I think of those who will sleep
in rows again, their white headstones
which someone else will keep clean.

*DENISE BENNETT*

# Nothing I love is rubbish

*After 'The Lovers (The Dustman)' by Stanley Spencer*

My hair is grey but you made it beautiful
with your dirty fingers. When I look back on our love
nothing is discarded, not the cracked red teapot,
not the empty jam tin, not the cabbage stalks.

Take these mucky cord trousers, held up with string.
They were everything. Take my spotted shirt,
too big for the arms that held you; or this enamel jug
that dangles from my hand.

O, my grubby love, how I dream of you,
of your weary, soiled body which I will carry
past the picket fence, the clipped peacock, the white dog,
the broken crockery, the green feathers of my old hat

towards the open cottage door,
that glint of firelight, those tied-back curtains,
the stone lintel, the latticed window,
the man with the beard who is always looking up.

*CAROLE BROMLEY*

# Golden Slumbers Sonia Rose

*After 'Hilda, Unity and Dolls', 1937, by Stanley Spencer*

has pits for eyes like her nameless sister doll.

Daddy never painted more than black holes
with darkest violet,

but see the care he poured into mine,
piercing with recrimination, or so he imagined,

and mummy's, half melted in bitterness, one angry,
bisected by an iron ring of spectacle frame,

the right only part visible, grieving:
ink on the decree absolute only three months dry,

but here on my lap sits same blue-eyed doll,
eighty years old at least, looking it

with time-tossed hair and eyelids that clack open, shut,
when I tilt her on the blanket laid across arthritic knees.

Sat up, she stares blankly as if still posed for daddy,
seeing and saying nothing about his expression.

*GRAHAM BURCHELL*

# Caught up in Stanley's Hair

He loves the hair; it nearly steals the focus
of the scene. Lush with portent and
projection: styled inside a resurrection plot
or lingeringly whittled from life,
it glows amid a welter of shades
and substance, never less than crowning glorious.

His hair enthrals, luxuriantly mopping brow
like an angelic choirboy caught in thought.
Its sheen and pile belie the careless toss of strands;
sharp trim betrays apparent ragged cut.
It draws the eye no matter where it falls:
at centre stage though nestled in arresting pose.

Inside a snood or half veiled by a hat
it hugs the head, almost pernickety
with finely chiselled artistry; the burnished waves
bounce light across the surface of the face,
and sparks of rawness hidden underneath
burn deep impressions smouldering beyond the frame.

Even the dustman's pate, archly wreathed
with sculpted leaves, gains sway through topiary:
green halo furnishes a kind of sanctity
amongst the rubbish bins, fondling with love
the greyness of his wife's familiar locks,
natural and free beside the coiffures of her friends.

To me it feels like Stanley celebrates head
over heart, the sensuality of all
the mind can forge above physicality.
Detail, rooted in the commonplace,
sets seedlings in a fertile soil
exploding to disseminate the sublime.

*LINDA BURNETT*

# An Incident in Cookham Churchyard

At first and last it looks quite ordinary,
as though upheavals such as this occur
on many Friday afternoons in June;
a blackbird's squawked alarm, but no last trump,
no seraphim, to herd the newly risen

into lines.

There in the middle,
gentle and absent minded, God
strokes His son's hair, while all around,
the residents of this home counties suburb
rub their eyes, stretch, clamber out of graves,
or raise whole clumps of daisied earth;
a wife pats down her husband's coat,
another reads a letter, or a will;
all pause, to get their bearings, reassess
this second coming.

Far left, along the tree-lined Thames,
a pleasure boat, weighed down
with tourists on a one day, one way
trip, drifts to the river's verge
to see, to share, this spectacle:
transposing time, and that once fixed
division of the earth and air,
the dead, the quick.

*JIM CAMPBELL*

# Zacharias and Elizabeth, 1914

An English offering. There in the top
reach of the home meadow, near where it shades
into the scrub as sleep folds into sleep,
he burns the scraps of lamb as one might burn
raked leaves – drawn down and sheepish while he feeds
the pale flesh to the flame. And his wife runs

to him, the rumour of new life in her
like talk of a new war passing from lip
to lip. "In these days he has shown his favour,
and taken away my disgrace" he thinks
picturing heaven's crisp ledgers. Men chop
wood, mend the hedges, build up the banks

set for the blessing of the October rain
that drops like a libation on the land.
Wind parts his wife's white hair and sends a skein
of thin smoke skirling skywards, and the small
girl sees all this, sees it and understands
that signs and wonders happen over the wall.

*ROSS COGAN*

# Deletions, Dear Desmond (August 1916)
## *or* Me, Today and Tomorrow

*The words in this poem are Stanley Spencer's own, distilled from a letter he wrote in 1916. See Note from the publisher, p.xx.*

Cookham Moor on a Tuesday afternoon.
Walking the Causeway is Dorothy Bailey;
How much Dorothy you belong
To the Marsh meadows and the old village.
I love your curiosity & simplicity, domestic Dorothy.

I hear the anvil in Mr. Lanes blacksmith shop
Shadowed by elms outside the red bricked wall.
Above the elms, Mr. Wallers malt houses
Slate roofs & heavenly white wooden cowls

An occasional young girl with some wreath
She is taking to her mothers grave.
New shoes on, all shiny black.
So unhappening, uncircumstantial & ordinary.

Mama safely packed off to Maidenhead
I let the bathchair swerve where it likes
Enjoy the eternal happiness of this life irrisponsible.

The children of the 'back-lane' school singing.
Mr. Tucks milk cart standing. Ice taken
Under the arch by Mr Caughts butchers shop,
Dragged along the ground by callipers.
He has an awful yet fascinating way of clutching ice.

I enter our house. Kitchen flooded with sunlight.
Plates and dishes on the tall dresser
Glisten sparkeling bright in the sunlight.
The shadow of the maid shifts about.

Into the dining room, the cloth is laid.
Sit down to the piano & look at my Bach Book.
Tea comes in. I take 3 pieces of bread and butter
And a big cup of tea. Then I have more.

Down our garden the yew tree has many apatures.
All seem holy and secret.

Turning to Sydney ask him to play some Preludes.
He does, though haltingly, with true understanding.

I go upstairs and think about the resurrection.
Get my big bible and read the Book of Tobit;
Gentle evening breeze through the open window
Slightly lifts the heavy pages.

I go through Cookham Church yard and pause
A tombstone railed round with iron railings.
To the right a mound guarded by two small firs.
I return and put it down on paper.

I think still more hopefully about the resurrection.
Not over satisfied with evenings thought,
But know that tomorrow will see the light,
Tomorrow 'in my flesh shall I see God'.

Sup cherries and custard with Mama.
To Annie Slacks shop and watch the customers.

Great doings of the night over and shops closed
One walk and the river moves on in solid mass.

Home and to bed. Crime and punishment
Under my arm and a candle which would last
A lifetime. After 2 or 3 hours blow out the candle,
And whisper a word to myself.
'Tomorrow' I say and fall asleep

*SHEZ COURTENAY-SMITH (EDITOR)*

# A Belfast Galleryman Speaks

*'The Betrayal' by Stanley Spencer (Ulster Museum)*

If I came to Cookham it wasn't
for the graveyard—youths
and their hiking partners busy
with rationed meat-paste
sandwiches among quiet prone
headstones I'd seen disgorge—
or to have him have us meet
faces I knew from walk-on parts
in his chaotic *Oberammergauen*:
I came for the garden shed,
the redbrick-topped wall
with Stanley and brother shrinking
away from the most awesome
apprehension in history.

Acquired before I got the job,
it spoke to a people who knew
the search party, *powers that be*,
Pharisees, (knew John 18:10
and the cutting off of ears better
than they knew Van Gogh's story
or John Ford's *Informer* though I'd see
in later years a corrugated shed
with *Judas was a tout* aerosolled).
It spoke to any small boy who'd shrunk
as I had from the sanguinary
of the backstreet police ambush.

He'd come often after the next war,
visited another brother's family,
paintings of Daphne, his niece,
or the lough's low foreshore.
Diminutive and voluble he showed me

how he worked sitting, floor-level,
eulogised Clydeside back-to-backs
where he'd lodged as war artist. Seemed
naïve to ask, as our gospel-savvy
populace all do, shuffling past,
*Why would he show Jesus there*
*stopping Simon Peter's sword*
*when we know all he could offer*
*was the healing business after?*

C.L. DALLAT

# Stanley Spencer Paints Christ

Four walls make a room.
This will do. I'll bar the door –
Live on bread and water. Forty canvases
Wait, whitely. They have lined themselves up.
The only flesh in here's my own –
I gulp and the air moves.

So now, oh Christ, I'll birth you in this
Cave, with this brush, this pallet.
Come now, into life, and may your
Gentle fatness feed me, your kindness
Spread beyond the square. Look – he comes –
From my brush tip
He comes, soft with love, supple, suppliant
Massive, with a laugh like thunder and a grip like rain.

Let no angels roll away the stone: it's he and I alone.

We begin to talk. We have the whole of Lent to thrash
The wilderness, to make something grow.

By the time I unlock the door, there'll be salvation.

*MIRANDA DAY*

# Christ in the Wilderness

*After Stanley Spencer*

the scorpion is all crescents
    sharp curve of horns
    pincertail
    armour arced into threat

Christ's hand is all pillows
plump fingers
palm cushioned as a quilt

beneath his feet
he feels the dry rasp of grit
and his own heaviness
as he squats
his whole body cupped
to this tight bend
    dull poke of spine
    against stretched skin
    the pull in the muscle
    a notquite pain

in this place full of brown stones
round as loaves
all his attention rests
in this moment
on this scorpion


and the scorpion    dances

*JAN DEAN*

# Nature and human nature: questions to Stanley Spencer

At Englefield, a single yew:
You painted it, and still the scene,
Seen by you, can charm us too.
To you, though, what did people mean?
Mean men, distorted by your eye –
I see no charm or kindness there.
Their limbs' proportions all awry,
A wry twist. So does what's laid bare
Bear witness to a tortured soul,
Sole saving grace beyond the grave?
Grave thoughts dispelled, as from earth's hole
Whole bodies rise – so faith will save?
Save for your vision of man's last hour,
Our hope and comfort: tree and flower?

*MARGARET DEUTER*

# Strawberry Moon

*After 'Self-Portrait with Patricia Preece', 1937, by Stanley Spencer*

This is Stanley's latest piece of nonsense,
*another fine mess*, as Mr. Hardy might say.

I didn't think his obsession with the Preece
creature would go this far, he's lost his house,

his money, and worst of all, me. I shan't
go back to Cookham, she can do whatever

she pleases with him. I don't know how
her devoted Dorothy puts up with this

farrago, but then, she lets Preece sign
& sell *her* paintings as by Patricia Preece.

Augustus John even called Preece one of
*the six greatest women artists in England.*

Typical. The old goat must be senile.
Anyway, the other goat, Stanley, comes

to me & blurts about marrying both of us
under the full moon in Glastonbury, says

there is a Strawberry Moon/Solstice conjunction
once every 70 years, we would be a holy triad

blessed by the full moon. Preece must have
cackled her way to the bank after writing

his script, and Dorothy looked the other way
as usual. I don't blame her for any of this.

BRIAN DOCHERTY

# Double Nude Portrait 1937

*'A Leg of Mutton' by Stanley Spencer*

Some nights he takes the canvas out
looks at it in a low light.
He crouches above her,
once more hoping
a shadow will soften
the unresponsive bodies,
the fire and meat become
an ordination of desire.

The man lingers upon the sex
and each stretch of skin.
But the painter notes how
the flesh of her thigh
rolls over the edge
of the frame,
escaping from his brush,
into a flight of life.

He cannot remember why she sat
for him silently detached;
but the taste of mutton,
its fat and grease, lingers;
the desire to eat
clogs his throat
like the sand and dirt
of a winter desert.

The skin of wounded men is soft
when he washes them;
the warmth recovered
Is the flush of nature.
But now he feels the gas heat
upon his back,
raw like the mutton
of a failed love making.
In those hospital beds there is

slack muscle and gristle
exposed and nurtured,
life restored or imagined
to resurrection, when, seeing
each as each,
those bodies will conjoin
as a river's shifting light.

But that was not his journey home.
So through each night
it haunts him unfinished.
The way out of paradise
is shaded with hope.
But the way back
is shadowed by ghosts
who hide the gate.

*ANDY DRAPER*

# Of Angels, Porcelain and Paint

*After 'Gardening', 1945, The Stanley Spencer Gallery*
*& 'Sunflower Seeds', 2010, by Ai Weiwei, Tate Modern*

Imagine a room, square windows
letting in the light. Imagine the light

is bright and yellow and falling
across rows of tables in slabs

the colour of butter. At the tables angels
are painting porcelain sunflower seeds –

the husks of sunflower seeds that is –
and, in the falling yellow light,

focus on a pigment each: pink, green,
russet, caramel, grey.

They take breaks at regular intervals,
stretch their necks and talk about the news –

somewhere a war is ending,
another about to start;

how it is they can survive all this.
And, on one particular, peculiar,

sun-drenched day Stanley comes,
and they give him their creations,

give him baskets brimming
with painted seeds for his collage

of two figures (daughter
and father) harvesting leeks.

He bends Kathleen to her task.
She can smell soap,

her father's gardener's skin
is surprisingly clean and,

if you listen carefully
you can hear a torrent of birdsong;

clouds are holding in the rain.
Imagine then you are walking

into the room with the square windows
and the light that's bright and yellow

and falling, and Stanley says,
*You can stir your fingers through the seeds*

*if you like, make billions*
*of shifting pictures, all uniquely yours.*

It will be like trying
to hold water in your hands.


*CLAIRE DYER*

# In Full Swing

*After 'Southwold', 1937, The Stanley Spencer Gallery*

There's no one in the water.
Even so the deckchairs

on lifeguard duty are
watchful, assiduous.

The sky's been stolen, been
carried away in a wicker basket

and the people have left
their faces at home.

If they could, they'd say,
*It's not easy walking here.*

Their footsteps have crafted
sand-and-shingle curls

between the breakwaters, windbreak and sea wall.

The waves balance the day
in their foam as a breeze

stirs the towels, salt crusts
onto bathing suits. I imagine

the sandwiches have meat paste
in them and the girl is reading

yesterday's news, but
can't decide if the shoes —

the wonderful shoes – hanging
on the line have been used

for running away from
or running towards.

*CLAIRE DYER*

# Scarecrow

Propped with a rust-patched stake
and a wooden pole, hoisted to my topmost,
thin ropes suspend arms that swim
through light all the more merciless
for being so cleansed.

Why is the compost heap covered
with a white cloth; is entombment
already waiting in the muck?

I am straw and striped shadow,
many-fingered right hand pointing
to my known future. Shrugging
where my face should be, I hide
beneath my black-banded hat.

Do I scare the birds? I only know
the sweet-peas whose pink, red
and yellow heads dart and tremble
in the breeze, a drunken fence
in the meadow, hazel sticks,
a clump of straw from my arm
snagged on bents, complete me.

Comfortable red homes that front
the woods as if they have always
been there, blush for my raggedness.
Everyone agrees crucifixions don't
take place in Cookham but I offer
my bonds to anyone who wants
to see me become one with the earth.

Soon villagers will march with pitchforks
and thrust them into my side
but no blood and water will pour. Mourners
will gather, Mary refuse to be comforted.
Always the same ritual of death and
unwanted resurrection.

*JOSH EKROY*

# Airmail

Dearest Stanley

I hope this finds you better
there's nothing left to say
but stop these endless letters
and paint my Stanley, paint

you'd love the boathouse Stanley
the river and the trees
the swans are angels all in pairs
betrothed eternally

there is a light here Stanley
a light that heaven sent
this warm expanse of endless love
speaks nothing of regret

H x

*MICHAEL FITZGERALD*

# And the trumpet shall sound

## One
with an indrawn breath,
with a scratch of air,
the sky goes white and crimped.

A bell sings.

Pigeons clatter out of the tower,
like applause;
crows from the elms,
a slap of wet sheets in a squall.

Then nothing.

The sky smooths its brow.
The birds settle.
The sun shines.

Stone grates against stone.
A stone falls with a dunt on the turf
Laurels and ivy sigh.

After a time, voices,
the trying out of tongues.
They say:           but

## Two

You know the dream;
that one when you're journeying
and hampered by the need to pack
you keep dropping things,
but you've got this urgent need to move
and there's the noise of something heavy
and the sky is lurching sideways
and you're blinking
thinking you can hear church bells, and you can,
and voices and the clatter of wings,
and there's a smell of cut grass,
and the sun is shining
and you're not dead
and so is everyone.
There's the cobbler you cuckolded,
the grocer whose small dog you kicked,
the wife you drank away,
the bookie who said he'd break your legs,
the publican whose slate you never paid,
the friends you bored,
all of them you thought you'd never see again
as you lay in the innocent dark.
Life after death.
Think on that.

*JOHN FOGGIN*

# how to make Saint Francis
# (and the birds): an origami poem

Take an empty square of land,
all ready, washed and white.

Begin by folding lengthwise, thus,
where the roof breathes at a fair, red tilt.

At the sunlit hour, press the sky
out on an upper crease,
and wait for the world to wake up, and go out.

Now you may make the Saint:
double back the belly-cord, and then unfold.
The fat smock will open
on a shadowed yard,
in which, from A to B, the beard will rise
like a hopeful, warmed meringue.

Begin with a bird-base.
Make a valley-fold, in whose bright homestead
nothing yet will speak: each beak,
and mouth, is winged and pressed still shut.

Repeat for poultry required, earth and roof.

To let all Heaven loose, align the creases
C and D, double back, and then unfold:

your birds will clatter forth, and scream,
and follow, thus, the fat gentleman,

who will bounce towards the trees,
with pop-up hands,
towards the Higher End,
and speak volumes.

These may be turned down,
by ruck and kink:
but who would want that?

Finally, turn the earth over,
with world-wide hands,
and cast all that you have
at the corn, and the meal,
and the shuffle-shoes;

at the words that are sung when the world unfolds,
and are silent asleep in the put-away sun,
but remain drawn unshut.

*JOHN GALLAS*

# On Reflection

*'The Harbour, St Ives', 1937, by Stanley Spencer*

How should the heart respond to tides that come
and go across a painter's sweep of shore?
Two palms stand sentinel: their tall fronds frame

a corner of this scene, with light so pure
that waves can all be counted as they fold
themselves around the bobbing yachts, which moor

inside the harbour. Shapes of liquid gold,
green, silver, white and Cornish blue spread out
in undulating patterns. Nets are filled

with notions of enchantment in the heat
of holidays, but castles in the sand
will disappear when sunset turns to night.

Atlantic ripples dazzle as they pound
the viewer's shore: how should the heart respond?

*CAROLINE GILL*

# Resurrection on Tewkesbury High Street

*After Stanley Spencer*

Then you and I let all impediments
fall, threw off the rags that covered our Eden;
and when I woke, people on the High Street
walked naked, stripped of the criticisms
we fasten to humans. They saw each other
as animals, or as lifted branches
that buckle under beauty: every deepening
arc of breast and belly found fellowship
in their slowly staged perfection of flesh,
every shoulder and hip angled in grace
for body to pass body, respecting
the narrow pavement, and the whole glad
consort carried all that it needed: bread
for morning toast, a little wine for dinner.

*HELENA GODDARD*

# Vardarec, Vardaris

Dear Stan
We write to take you out of that zone of yours into ours,
That which you entered, oh so briefly, in your Sixteen
And which you sought to capture with your brush for ever more.
To Yockney you wrote of depicting the scene at Smol
Without, as you said, 'truthfully representing' what you'd seen.
Oh, how we admire your honorable artistic goal.
Let us tell you first, that wounded are still arriving... and
    departing
At our place, which shortly after your time here
Greek officials renamed Mikro Dasos, your Little Wood.
Stan, we've admired your icon with its order but no stasis.
You are right to have placed us in the dress circle of your theatre
For from in, and as, the gods, we, like you, see further than stalls,
    wings and stage.
Indeed we safely observe the enigma of arrival in your
    thanatopolis
Because you've also put us out, above and beyond the phrygana
That trails across your eery elision of interior and exterior.
Just remember, for all your record of noble, peaceful, pain
That muleteer you moaned of arms that ached from lugging
And cried out for moving, materials, change.
You call the Battle of Machukovo an attack on Machine Gun Hill,
While the 'never ending stream' of casualties you noted
Were more than two battalions lost to German force... and history.
Your colours and lines bleat redemption, offer hope
But since you're working for the Ministry we'd like some faces,
Please give us names, if not of those who sent and went, at least of
    those so rent.
For all your invaluable recollection, we know but one:
Dear Ernest Grace, a young private of the Lancashire Fusileers,
Killed in Evzonoi action beneath us, Vardarec-Vardaris.
Meanwhile, we'll give you a taste of our domain of river, knoll
    and air

With its vast necropolis of duo kiloyears past
And Hellenist idol of the ancients' god of archery, art and poetry.
Bulgar Smolikas was Ottoman, the Smolioti under a Turkish bey.
As the Sick Man weakened and other Sick Men meddled
Our place became a beating heart of Macedonian being and
 becoming.
Still its aorta was severed, first by the Sionidis gang, then the
 Bashibazouks.
Here, just before your dressing station days, were dozens of cheta
 slaughtered
And Apostol, liberation leader, among the few left wounded.
Then, after you'd gone, this place turned Hellas
With Sarakatsani set and Pontics resettled, the last
Survivors of Young Turk wipeout policies further east.
Now in your dressing place are temples of Pantaleon and Taxiarchis
And nearby is a border, with Bogoroditsa on the other side, Idomeni
 on this:
Great Healer, Bodiless Commander, Mother of God, Seer of Force.
Alas, in our Sixteen, we're back to soldiers and stretchers a-coming,
Doctors, nurses, volunteers and camps of caught-up multitudes:
The fare of far-off major wars of more Sick Men's making.
In ending, Stan, we thank you for your vision of sacrifice, deliverance.
You've harkened folly, violence and compassion.
Through your artifice travoys, table, actors carry moment.
We call on those who know and love you
To read beyond your orderly lines and repetitions
So that all may comprehend the cycles of man's waging.
Stan, for the sake of puny man, hear, be touched by, and feel us.
All around you and yours, we are the wind of all... and nothingness


*JACEY GOMME*

# Spencer, Private no. 40812, C Company

*I could be content to speake of this Resurrection by the low way
of the grave, till God by that gate of earth, let us in at the other*
—Donne, Sermon XIX

In the eye of the storm, the Balkan states,
there's no storm. I watch the sun stub its woodbines
on the mountain ridges. All night a line
of ants has spooled out from my mess-tin
back to its trench. Soon small lizards will flash
from their dug-outs and pick them off. What grass
there is here grieves in the shadows. Too dry
for sowing, but the topsoil loosens easily.
A run-dry pond blisters under a scab of scree.

Before the sun reaches our outpost I
have three graves to open. Three dead men
sprawled under tarp since yesterday when
the packed mules budged down from the horizon:
barbed-wire Xs shifting across my
field of vision. All blown by the same mine,
crumpled almost into one mess of limbs.

Grave-fatigue, hatching into the hillside a few scores, untangling a pile of
crosses. Dig deep and pile up infill,
stick my spade on the top and cough.

I put them into piles, hold their burst heads.
The parts of them are lowered. Prayers are said.
Then the sun kicks down on us mulishly.
I spade the topsoil back in place. I won't re-

member this. More than bodies are being
buried. Dispositions of arms, heaving
trenched legs that won't climb back to heaven,

if that exists. Pack them down under
memory, under standing. Block the well
with my blunt spade. There is a hell
bruised inside this hill like fossil water.
It will clarify almost into air.

When evening light starts to mend the sky I'll
fill my helmet at the spring and lie still.
Later I may remember how the mule's
ear twitched, and with oil on canvas show you
can't open a door unless you've closed some first.
Show soldiers waking, rising, time reversed.
How sleeping and living are warring states.

*GILES GOODLAND*

# St Francis and the swimmer

Stanley Spencer, son of a man whose trousers were stolen
who then walked around Cookham in his dressing gown.
There is something heartwarming about this story.
The son later recalled his father, untrousered,
fetching poultry feed from the alleyway larder.

After Giotto,
this simple scene needed attentive wild birds
to lend it old meaning. Some chickens sufficed,
and some geese and two ducks. Ecce!
St Francis. And the Birds.

From the father's billowing body, the doubled head,
the turned around feet, the oddly thumbed hands,
emerges a soon-to-be-split mirrored image
of William-St-Francis.

St Francis will silently pass through the glass to the past,
as William's luminous spirit returns to the present.
All the limbs that we see are his, not the saint's.
There is no anatomical flaw, only a conjurer's ruse

with perspective. William must rise through the final tidal ebb of his life,
and the seemingly unjointed arms, those hands, cannot be faulted
if seen as the sweeping force of a surfacing swimmer,
a swimmer who raises his face to his home.
Those arms, those hands, are his.

This is the way the son sees his father, a swimmer,
rising alone out of the deep, resolute and courageous.
The sea that he swims through is the soil of the grave.

Stanley is in the picture too, as a boy,
a time when his well loved father was still living.
So now he paints yet another Resurrection,
to bring a phantom, a man, back from the dead,
to scatter love for that boy like birdseed.

Hilda is also there, distressed and defensive.
Have plans for a ménage à trois been newly proposed?
Are the cut flowers she convulsively clutches his memories –
her memories – of her bridal bouquet?

The year was 1935. Stanley was bewitched by a woman
who later would very nearly castrate him. Patricia Preece.
She stole from her lover, Dorothy, recognition and fame.
She stole from Hilda her marriage and maybe her mind.
She stole from Stanley his house – his home – and his freedom.

Yet he still viewed the world through a prism of love,
for family and Cookham, for God, for Hilda,
for other women. He was liberal with his love.
Brave and unblinking, he painted that world.
Nothing was censored; nothing was hidden

We see him squatting, naked, abased, subjugated,
beside the nude, and bored, ambiguous Patricia.
We see his limply dangling
penis.

But art was his constant, consoling companion,
though landscapes had no role in that passion.
He mass-produced them to settle his debts. He claimed.
Yet he painted the meadows and woods of a magical world
with the fealty of a pre-Raphaelite, and his own distinct vision of truth.

*MARYLOU GRIMBERG*

# Resurrection

*"As my soul shall not go towards heaven, but go by heaven to heaven."*
*John Donne, Sermon XLVI*

And what if it's no more than the sudden breath
in a shallow dream, when you trip and reach
out a hand to break your fall and wake, a blood-
beat from first sleep? And what if the winding cloth
is no more than this white bedsheet on which
our bodies move together like weeds in Thames mud,
your hair in my mouth, onion tang of your breasts.
And later, when you rise and stoop to open a drawer,
take out a petticoat – a movement I have witnessed
some thousand mornings, I could not swear
whether this room belongs to the kingdom of heaven
or the kingdom of earth, or know to paint the distinction.

Five decades have died in this flesh, their memorials
these liver spots and callouses, the varicose vein
whose path I trace with my tongue along your thigh,
the belly's silver lines, dirt beneath our nails
from weeding between rows of tipsy columbines.
All these worldly flaws we regret or disguise
under stockings and coats will travel with us below,
where we shall look on them with new tenderness.
See now – the light that makes the curtains glow
might be the familiar old sun that wakes us
to another dawn of dying, or the final ray,
first salute to the last and everlasting day.

*EMMA HARDING*

# Ottolenghi's Feast

*After 'The Last Supper', by Sir Stanley Spencer, CBE, R.A,*
*The Stanley Spencer Gallery*

It could be fancy dress, the guests disguised
in dreadful wigs and shapeless shifts.

The maitre d' has told the waitresses to serve:
feta globes with olives from The Garden
soused in a virgin oil.

Unused to Michelin fare the faithful's hands have
grown too large, their words clag up their tongues.

Somewhere unseen a one star chef is turning up
the heat in preparation. Beneath the table diners
stretch their legs.

Only their feet, free and freshly washed, appear content.
They fold them as an angel folds its wings.

*HILARY HARES*

# Stanley Spencer at Cookham on Thames

*I.m. Carol Hogben*

As the river mist lifted each morning
Stanley saw the shrouded men and women
becoming clearer, rounder, coloured – living –
and the village rise in daily resurrection.

*MARK HAWORTH-BOOTH*

# The burial of Stanley Spencer

*For Edwina Cooper*

The painter's burial took place
in December 1959
and a man much later recalled
how he, a chorister, was present
when earth was tossed on the coffin
and wind gusted through
the churchyard catching
the choir's surplices and blowing
them all in one great white
shape across the grave —
which is how a flight of angels
sang the painter to his rest.

*MARK HAWORTH-BOOTH*

# Two Paintings of Hilda Carline

*(i)  Hilda by herself*

'*In your painting I can understand and love you.*'
Did Stanley love you in this spinster bedroom,
with its homely patchwork quilt? We know
he didn't. Still, your hopes were high. You meet
our gaze with almost confidence under your fawn
felt hat. You don't yet know the paint box at your side
(which stakes your claim in this family of painters
to be taken, although a woman, seriously)
will have to be unpacked and then abandoned
in a bedroom just like this, where the child sleeps
and Stanley complains of the dreary beating of tin cans
that accompanies the symphony of his work.


*(ii)  Hilda and Stanley*

The newlyweds have taken the hotel by surprise.
Nothing is ready. We can see the waitresses
scramble to lay a cloth, while the only bridesmaid
leans in to ogle the wedding cake, a phallic
helter-skelter of royal icing set before the groom.
With her back to us Hilda smooths her white
satin skirt a moment before she settles, like
a swan touching water. Mild faced, straining
the line of his arm and shoulder, Stanley
has painted himself pulling her chair away.

*MAEVE HENRY*

# Just a minor detail

They are old now, these Sandham trees.
Wooden props take the strain
while apples fall and soon will be
lost to an early morning frost.
And the crosses spangle and pile
like the jacks of giants, now the men
reclaim their scraped and bitten feet,
reach across with blood-warmed hands,
trying to recall
        where they had left themselves:

white as sacrifice,
white as a winter dawn trailing
its hoary breath over Salonika.
Was it only the Christ man keeping watch
as they pick over these bones of restitution,
fighting to remember whose weight
it was they had come to carry,
whose empire they were shoring up?
Just a minor detail
        in this not-for-promised land.

*KAREN IZOD*

# Still here

The angels are wearing badges now,
beautiful pewter signs of greeting,
*welcome! welcome!* Or else those plastic
holders of identities that say we are carers,
we care for you, as you grow old in frame,
rise in stature, as your hearts lift
to the bells pealing out across the pasture
where I wanted to lie down with You,
but had to wait, and instead bathed
those feet in a flush of sunlight, seven
pairs, under the table, their twisted toes,
interlinking as a matter of faith,
as though we knew time was short.
Man hath such a short time.

Down at the Ferry Inn, the waiters are tending
their flock with cappuccini, *mind they don't spill,*
stirring memory in the time-honoured way,
*eat this, drink this.* The water washes
high against the path as the trippers cruise by.

*Can you do swans?* the visitor asks
the tattoo artist, newly set up
from his caravan in the car park,
but wishing he was out with a handcart.
*I want a swan on each arm, necks twisting
around my biceps, so their wings tuck
up on my shoulders, and their beaks point ...*
where? He hasn't thought that far.
And his girlfriend, her arms warm and doughy,
asks for a magnolia, flushing pink
over her magnificence. He worries
about the permanence, the commitment
of the ink, the necessity of leaving
some Things undone.

*KAREN IZOD*

48

# Sewing on a Button

*'all ordinary acts such as sewing on a button are religious things
and a part of perfection...' Stanley Spencer*

She sucks the frayed cotton
so it will pass more easily
through the eye.

This is the eye of heaven.
Camels buckle to their knees.
Pans, fish crates, sacks of learning

crash to the ground. The button
is all that is missing from our lives.
All that is mislaid, forgotten. Love

left by the wayside. She passes her needle
through the holes a dozen times,
once for each disciple.

Winds round the base, sews through
with one cross, cuts the thread
with her teeth. The button holds.

Adam fastens his jacket. It is the first day.
We don our Sunday best —
collars, cuffs. It is the last.

Next door, the man hammering
a nail is from Palestine.
The woman carrying their child

is, perhaps, the mother of God.
The artist who pushes a pram
of paints down the High Street

is helping to coax the world
into being every moment —
*now*. And again *now*.

She threads another needle.
Her thimble pushes the light.
She stitches the world together.

*ROSIE JACKSON*

# The Heaven that Runs through Everything

Here's to the small everyday miracles –
Mrs Baggett with her knitting and pearls,

the lovely daughters of Jerusalem
in their gardens of lilies, laburnum,

gospels and gossip at the regatta,
Sarah Tubb and her heavenly visitor,

courting and baptism along the Thames,
a dustman leaping into his wife's arms.

Here's to tulip, rock rose, gypsophila
flowering together, to vases of prayer,

Saint Francis in slippers and dressing gown
up on the roof with hens to catch the sun,

chores doing themselves down in the kitchen
at a wedding where water's turned to wine,

everything married to everything else –
yearning to show itself as happiness,

as Love. Neighbours who rejoice with tin cans
and cabbage leaves, the ripe summer commons,

skies which open over bulrush, goose-run,
the fresh light making everything new-born,

shot through with flame, each shrub a burning bush
by the tow path. All detail the flourish

of nature to show itself exactly –
not 'bird' but swan, cockerel, grebe, quail, turkey.

Blessings on Ricket's Farm, Rowborough, Pound Field,
the very word 'Eden' changed, now *this* world

is all we need to know of paradise.
Consider the gardens at Cookham Rise

where Adam's walking backwards to a tree
laden with unpicked apples – the first day

and the last become one, as if heaven was
wanting to reveal its eternal *Yes* –

earthly desire become beatitude,
everything known to be equally god.

Suffering a page to be folded over,
tenderness up sleeves in the tents of war,

balm poured from seraphs in the guise of men.
Nothing that is not transfiguration –

the dying girl next door raised up, restored
to life, then the quickening of a horde

of spirits, hungry for what death waylaid –
the lost embrace, words not said, love not made.

Here's to grief unlearnt, grateful breath redrawn,
the rapture of rolling away the stone.

And let's not forget the man most at home
in sunlight, newly arrived in Cookham,

who walks with disciples up Cockmarsh Hill,
everyone in the crowd a plump angel.

*ROSIE JACKSON*

# Bedridden

Father calls
Capernaum fades
hands
grasp me

tiles clatter
joists snap
dust billows
stop ye I wail

no words come

below the breach
my weary limbs dangle
into tumult
fallen

unkempt stranger bends down
son you are forgiven
up I leap
roaring.

*PAUL JEFFCUTT*

# Elements

First is earth
        heavy flesh
second rock
        steadfast bone
third water
        blood fount
fourth salt
        whet nerve
fifth sky
        gust breath
sixth sun
        kindle heat
seventh spirit
        spark and star.

*PAUL JEFFCUTT*

# Blue Doughnut Annunciation

*14th Century Room, Ashmolean*

*OK*, she says.
She's just got up
from an after-lunch nap,
*God wants me*
*to have his baby.*
*That's cool.*

Not a, *What the Hell*
*do you imagine*
*my father will say?*
*Pull the other one, Girlie!*
or, *You must be joking!*
*The whole town will*
*call me a slut.* Not even,
*Joseph will hit the roof.*
Just, *OK, that's cool,*
and a mildly astonished, *Oh*
when the angel arrived
(as they do), as you do. Nice
hat feathers; nice doughnut halo,
nice coming and going into
the big golden tea-time
of a Nazareth afternoon.

*She's done it, God,* (to the sound
of tambours, timbrels and trumpets).
And God rolls off, a bit
smug, on his chariot,
in his papal tiara (already...?)
borne up by a few seraphim;
the ones that keep covering
their faces, but still manage
to see where they're going.

And Mary goes back to her book.

*HELEN KIDD*

# A long way from home

These too were God's creatures but alien as wildebeest
or orang-utans: rough skins, savage cries that rose
above the skreel of drills. Curious at first, the Jimmies,
Fergies, Ecks, soon let him be; their bonnie lassies
smiled him in, served him real men's food; their wains
listened goggle-eyed to his 'wireless' speech.

For weeks, eardrums throbbing to the driving-in
of rivets, clang of bruised steel, with spectacles ablaze
he sketched furnace fury, sprays of sparks, and workers
forging and forming panels, girders, pipes, then
like brawny ants, assembling their vast Meccano sets.
Near Lithgow's yard the Clyde unfurled, its firth so wide
that Cardross Hills were often lost. Cookham must
have seemed as hazy as a half-remembered dream.

*GILL LEARNER*

# Roy

## (b.1902, d.1910)

*(on a pen and ink drawing, c 1907, made
when the artist was fifteen/sixteen)*

Just being there, small boy against
A low, dark-boarded pew his arm
Could rest elbow-to-shoulder on,
The way they did, forearm along
A bit, hand down the other side.
His face is looking out, away.

What Stanley was drawing here would be,
So soon, dear memory: Roy's cheek,
An ear, light rough-cut hair , his suit,
Socks slipping down, his shoes drawn small,
Legs smaller than they should have been.

So this is all. He did not come
With others *rising* on that day
In Cookham churchyard. Close to home,
A child, he could not find his way.

*JOHN LOVEDAY*

# The Resurrection, Cookham

*Stanley Spencer*

My wayward aunt, who claimed to be his cousin,
once confided that this picture caused
some scandal in the village. Stanley had shown
couples rising up, embracing the wrong partners,
hinting at local gossip, known affairs.

I love the notion, though I have my doubts.
She could be provocative in telling tales –
like one about the conjuring brother, Horace,
their drinking in the Riviera bar
together on the night that he was drowned.

As others of our family, she'd grown up
among those ample women in bold frocks,
the awkward men made fluid in check suits,
who did their work, made love, and acted out
the Bible's passions on his village street.

Strange, now, to come across them in
hushed galleries, haloed in tasteful light,
incongruous, as the artist may have been
in China, or arriving at the Palace
with his shopping bag and paint-flecked suit.

If they returned today, those churchyard couples,
they might find their village looked familiar
though had nowhere you could buy fresh bread,
a mutton chop – processions, rather, of tourists
looking for echoes of the daily lives they'd led.

*TONY LUCAS*

# Redemption

*After 'The Resurrection of The Soldiers' by Stanley Spencer*

I've buried too many to paint them dead.
    Each day the wounded arrive on travoys
        we welcome them with sandwiches and tea

We scrub floors, launder sheets and shirts, rejoice –
    this drudgery our tribute to fallen
        comrades. Look, God is in all things I love

death is not an end, I paint in hope. So
    row on row of neat white crosses break rank
        pushed up from the ground by soldiers re-born.

Eager to start their day's work they help mates
    escape the sepulchral clay (a sombre
        palette of umber, blue ochre, green earth).

Animals too, not forgotten, rise and
    straighten limbs that have been awry in death
        and men read their names on their own headstones,

amazed to find they have been dead and now
    are here, shaking each other by the hand.
        They pass round wire cutters, roll up puttees

buff their buttons; carry their crosses up
    Machine Gun Hill – hand them to the waiting
        Christ who has had this joyful second thought.

*CHRISTINE MACFARLANE*

# Family Portrait

*After 'Family Group: Hilda, Unity and Dolls', 1937,*
*by Sir Stanley Spencer*

This is too close-up. Look
into the painting, you feel
like a voyeur intruding at
an intimate, difficult moment.

She will not catch your eye
Hilda, behind her heavy glasses
and turns deliberately away.
The child though, gazes out.

Who are you? She seems to ask
yet she stares at her father as he
paints them into this corner of
a room in the family home.

The dolls, he paints without eyes.
Is this in threes, you think – eyes
averted, eyes ahead, and those
with no eyes? Or has he had enough

of stares? Cannot bear the glassy
judgement of these pretend-people,
in cahoots with their daughter;
dreads the click made, as their eyes

fall closed. All she ever wanted
was this – children, art, being
together. But out of this frame
he's lost to them. In an agreed

cease-fire, she sits for him
once more; wears her green in
silence, loses herself. Knows
he will make a masterpiece

of all the surfaces he sees –
the white splashes on Unity's frock,
each hair of her own head,
the ruched stitching at her shoulder,

He's always been good at surfaces.

*CHRISTINE MACFARLANE*

# A Disciple views Stanley Spencer's
## *Last Supper*

Yes, those are my feet.
Our Teacher washed them.
They had never felt so clean.

Nathanael and I had to grip
the table for fear of floating away.
They crossed of their own accord.

Whatever was going on in our heads
our feet were at peace. As you can see
there were the usual tensions.

Peter objecting, then relenting,
then going overboard. Judas
up to something. A sense of endings.

To be honest, after he touched my feet
I wasn't very present.
My right ankle had troubled me

since I twisted it as a child
but its ache had lifted.
When he swaddled them

in the towel at his waist
I was back at my mother's breast.
I would never go hungry again.

My mind was in my feet.
They could take me anywhere,
I could stand in front of anyone

and speak of my Master.
Yes, those are my feet
full of goodness and strength.

*LORRAINE MARINER*

# Christ in the wilderness

Rising from sleep in the morning, I am
a flower diving into day. Though petals fade
and seed is scattered, I am unafraid
in the solitude of this steep mountainside
where even my breath is shallow,
sight stretched far.

No lilies bloom here; I've left behind the hen
whose encircling care reminded me of God's
maternal love; I've even lost the foxes —
playful triangles that kept my loneliness at bay.
Who or what can keep me company here?
Only eagles that attack and eat their prey.

Don't blame me; I didn't choose to favour an eagle
over a gazelle, would rather feed them both with milk
of human kindness, or even my own flesh. Don't you
understand the birds must eat? They take no pleasure
in this carnage, are just being what they were made to be —
not tame and satisfied, but wild, hungry and free.

I'm driven into this wilderness to pray,
and in my palm I hold a scorpion, or it holds me.
Sadness threatens to overwhelm, but still
I struggle to offer this small creature
my loving contemplation, even though
its tail is raised to sting, perhaps to kill.

*ALWYN MARRIAGE*

Christ in the wilderness comprises eight paintings: *Rising from sleep
in the morning,* 1940; *He departed into a mountain to pray,* 1939;
*Consider the lilies,* 1939; *The hen,* 1954; *The foxes have holes,* 1939;
*The eagles,* 1943; *Driven by the spirit into the wilderness,* 1942;
*The scorpion,* 1939

# Cookham to Bristol Mental Asylum

## (1 day/89 miles/walking)

High Street, School Lane to Maidenhead Road
Cannondown Road, back to Switchback Road

Malders Lane, through to Winter Hill Road
Golden Ball Lane, then Marlow Road & Darlings Lane

Henley Road, then to Burchetts Green Lane
Bath Road, then London Road, then Bath Road again

Pincents Lane, High Street – Church Street (pray)
The Green, Bath Road again, up Benham Hill

Hawthorn Road, Chestnut Crescent (arboretum)
Western Avenue, to Salisbury Avenue, then George Lane

Pewsey Road & Bridewell Street, then Eastern Avenue
Cocklebury Road, up Station Hill to the Road (new)

Marshfield Road to Bristol Road & Siston Common
Station Road, up Teewell Hill to Broad Street

High Street (again), then Fishponds Road to Manor Road
& the Blackberry Hill Hospital.

*STEPHEN JAMES MOORE*

Stanley Spencer b. 30 June 1891 d. 14 Dec 1959
English Painter, Cookham, Berks.

# Golden Slumbers Sonia Rose

*After 'Hilda, Unity & Dolls', 1937, by Stanley Spencer*

He blackens, brushes out sockets, buries their gaze,
turns hope away like Hilda's, yet finds in Unity
the clarity of an unswerving stare. She holds me,
her childhood doll, preserved into old age,
the memory of our Unity, unsullied, pure.

These blue glass eyes close and open wide,
still sighted in her cradling arms.

*JILL MUNRO*

# I am nothing like domestic

When my neighbour kisses me
I often forget the surprising third
the cheeky one that says *I'm Dutch*.

After, Jan tells me he misses real
Gouda, cumin seeded in green rind
cinnamon biscuits at Christmas time
dark wheat beer, and thin light
in a vast cloud sky.

That's why his good wife plants
tulips, wax lips to blaze and crazy
their river garden in spring on days
when I don't cut the privet, leave it
for nesting birds.

Did I say he's fond of swan's down?

Handed over the hedge, my reward's
a bunch of scarlet. It burlesques
my kitchen table, petals flash
black triangles as lifted skirts
pollen teases the oil skin cloth.

*KATE NOAKES*

# Approaching Heaven

*After 'Cookham Moor', 1937, by Stanley Spencer*

His is the view this runner saw
approaching Cookham from the Moor,
the High Street hushed as first birds called —
lovers and angels still asleep.

He said ...*heaven was to one side*\*
and, running through just after dawn,
the supernatural lingered still
round corners, behind hedge or wall.

His visions people this small place —
those paintings were his main concern;
the landscapes, like this *Cookham Moor*
he scorned – made for commercial gain.

Yet in this view I find my past —
those Sunday runs more special now,
memories of my feelings, how
I felt the spirit of this place.

If I could do that run today
would Spencer›s visions haunt me still?
Or spectre, with a paint-smeared pram —
a silent presence on this road...

*PATRICK OSADA*

---

\*   Gilbert Spencer said that Stanley... 'had the idea that heaven was
    to one side: walking along the road he turned his head and looked
    into heaven.'

# Balkan September

*Travoys Arriving with Wounded*
*at a Dressing-Station at Smol, Macedonia*

Burnt landscapes recur
and we're crossing again
disputed territory
where not so far from here
the bodies on their way home
were to be assessed
in that war to end all wars'
relentless triage.

Once seen, perhaps,
this palette remains
unavoidable –
the dun and ochre hills
recede towards prospects
of a victory it took more
than parades and flags
for you to survive.

Not that fig trees
behind closed walls
are giving much away,
being part of a scenery
that takes us about as far
as we can get from a faith
which, on the face of it,
might make things cohere.

At a roadside stall,
they're talking again
of embroidery and feuds –
or that's what we assume,
being no more at home
than you were then
in heat and mud,
the savagery of guns.

Echoes of which ...

Echoes of which
now sound in reports
of a stand-off
not so far from the border.
The intervening terrain
crackles and flakes
like damaged paint,
a blistered surface.

Something more
to be found, observed
in the broiled atmosphere
is what we can hope for,
though lines, planes retreat
into the dusk – as we do
while this man shines
his torch across our passports.

*TOM PHILLIPS*

# Flood

A new sound welcomed us as
We turned the little boat into
The lane. A hollow thud against
The hull, followed by two more.

Caught between tall, bare hedgerows
Small red signposts, leading the way
Along the mirror lane.
Breaking the surface we pushed,
Through thuds and clunks, toward the farm.

He waited, crouched on low flat roof.
Watching for our approach. The yard
Glowed a bright red blaze in winter sun.
The mud brown tide hidden beneath
A thousand apples, gently
Washing back and forth from gate to barn.

Tied around his neck by the laces,
A pair of patent brogues.
Without fingerprint or smudge
To ruin the deep black shine.
'Not much to show for a life'.
He said as he climbed into the boat.
'Just a suitcase and two pair of shoes'.

*CHARLIE PLEDGER*

# The Deposition and Rolling away of the Stone

*After Stanley Spencer*

The need for geometries, correct
instrumentation; the body aligned
precisely, pinned and mounted
on wood with right hammer

and good nails. The taking down
of same: how one might stoop
to the task, squint into the flesh
to get the exact purchase, which pliers

would extract the nails most effectively,
how to lever and jemmy appropriately.
And how it sounds; the nails
squeeze from the wood, the flesh

slipping from the upright, the feet
with their slight woosh of parting;
anticipation of stone rolling upon
stone at the entrance to the tomb.

*IAN POPLE*

# In the detail

*Map Reading 1932*

You're caught in the act, looking down at your map.
You think you know the way to the next part of the war;
how the war will run its course, and the reasons for it all.

There are rivers in your hands – forests, mountain ranges;
you think you have knowledge, you are the man in charge,
for God is an Englishman, so the world is in your grasp.

Soldiers lie on the grass; gazing upwards at passing suns,
while the Earth breathes out small statements of intent,
which fall as damp ashes on the veracity of your map.

Men troop in a line, as if someone knows the way inside
luscious bushes, as fleecy as home horse-chestnut trees.
They stretch out their bodies, reaching up for bilberries.

*VICTORIA PUGH*

# Southwold 1937

God Stanley's on the prom.
He knows a thing or two.
But he's not telling you.

The windbreak's bulging.
A towel on a line flicks
its tongue in anticipation.

The sea's oozy. Its crusty
light keeps breaking up:
summer dazzling ice floe.

Light drips on a book, each
half-pebble, a hat; the sea-
wind bronzes everything.

Here, take this deckchair –
its mouth is wide enough
for everyone to sit there.

Rest, in this lit-up hollow
way, this dry gap in a wet
stone wall, this cure-all.

God Stanley couldn't stay.
He left this for you: come
on in – it's lovely in here.

*VICTORIA PUGH*

# Double Nude Portrait of the Artist and His Second Wife

## (The Leg of Mutton Nude)

*A painting by Stanley Spencer, 1937*

It only occurred to him late, days
into her pose on the striped duvet.
He'd had to find the correct position
for the arms, now overhead, barely

half in frame. And sorrow, or the soul-filled
look beyond of her gaze, and the full
sag of each breast along the ribs, the bony
pelvic rise, and her colour of leaves.

He'd solved the problem of his body
in the scene, hands tucked under like Mary's
holding Christ. He saw at last the meat too
made sense beside them, a third holy thing.

*RICHARD ROBBINS*

# Christ Carrying the Cross

*A painting by Stanley Spencer, 1920*

And we saw someone passing below,
we who jammed the sash of each high window
like twins sprouted from a common waist.
And it was the quiet work below

we noticed first, something no one called
suffering, though it seemed what we'd been called
to bear. We watched ladders, crooked hands, heard
talk proceed as always, saw through old

remarkable eyes. Why, then, be startled
to find ourselves winged, some changed world
in the making along ivy and brick?
Someone pulled that slow cross to a hill.

*RICHARD ROBBINS*

# Resurrection

There is no silence in the grave
old roots heave and sigh;
all you had is lost, surrendered
all you were, has seeded back through time

There is no peace within the grave
cold rains drill, then flood
till you are sunk, made faceless
redemption lying deep below the mud

There is no resting in the grave
clay thuds dull and faithless
yet death is not our last landscape
and graves cannot contain us

*KIM ROONEY*

# The Suit of Stars

The man with a suit made of stars
juggles an apple in one hand,
and with the other switches on

the darkness – he's taking us back
to the millisecond the universe began
and our atoms were the smoke,

apocalyptically gold, on dawn's fields.
He walks us deeper into the night
and we feel the freezing air coming in

from the cosmos, drenching our bones.
By now we're ready to believe anything.
That our little lives will find a space

big enough to hide in, that a tiny spark
will leap the gap, that our sounds will carry;
that these green-blue hills will dwindle and fall

and rise again long after our children's
children's children; that a grizzled skipper
will alight for an instant in the copper tree.


*LESLEY SAUNDERS*

# Air and Angels

Rabbits frolic, playing families. A squat
    Doric temple sits chalky-white and proud
on a furrowed hill, the only pilgrim
    a farmer on a tractor, his straw hat
squinting out from the prophetic cloud
    of ninety-nine gulls transfiguring him.

Badgers wrestle in a ditch. A fieldfare
    flock feasts on berries in a rowan tree
tingling with dew. And now, like an angel,
    precipitate in the autumnal air,
an idea forms, which helps good souls to see
    how angels might be more corporeal.

If the temple frieze has four sets of scenes
    sculpted upon its metopes (let's say,
the arts, religion, war and industry),
    common sense tells us of a human means
of contemplating this entire array
    of the state of England with godlike eye

from just one place: that is, to exhibit
    the four friezes round the walls of a room
in a gallery, turning them outside in
    to let the pilgrim view them inside out,
as if the Redeemer from His broken tomb
    had shown us how our gladness might begin –

how, over English fields and hedges, seven
    angels in woollies and pleated skirts, hair
nicely done, might fly with flasks of seeds,
    tilting them to broadcast hopes of heaven,
red linings hidden like the humblest prayer,
    the spiritual undersides of earthy tweeds.

*ROBERT SAXTON*

# The Silent Collection

*After 'The Dustman' or 'The Lovers' by Stanley Spencer*

Every day the dustman forgets himself
in cleansing labour, in his striped jersey,
brown corduroy trousers and black beret.
Every night he forgets himself in love.

He's not unhappy with his earthly lot:
it's just that he's ambitious for more bliss –
more life in every dustbin, every kiss,
a stronger infusion in the moment's pot.

Like love affecting everything we do,
home taken to a finer point of feeling
distils not downwards from a mystic ceiling
but outwards from the useful and the true.

Good things discarded years before their time
may still disclose their lustre through life's grime.

                    *

On collection day bystanders gather round
the dustman ecstatic in his wife's embrace,
her love for him so strong with erotic grace
she lifts him, like a child, right off the ground.

As if waiting their turn, the others watch
in two little clusters, male and female,
patient for their destiny to prevail,
the consummation of a spotless match.

Each loves the rest, in an atmosphere
of joy as peaceful as the privacy
of a lavatory. Such blessed intimacy!
Bored with hopscotch, the dustman's kids appear,

diving into bins for a fitting homage:
old teapot, empty tin, limp leaves of cabbage.

*ROBERT SAXTON*

# First

thing in the morning you'd light up the fire. You'd lift up the rivet, sink it into the char and blow till they got red hot then white hot and then it started fizzing and then you'd shove it in the hole and my jacket had a hole burnt through by a fleck of iron as hot as the sun.

Look, this is me crouching inside the steel pipe. He sketched me here in the shipyard. He was squatting on the ledge of the platform, half lost in white-hot bolts from the furnace. He had a teapot on the ledge. And he did a drawing of welders with blowtorches hoisted like spacemen. *Like angels*, he said, *peering down their visors on the earth below*.

But the noise just knocked you crazy and you were so black with grime and oil and all that. Wait, this is the old wood-working machine, and these parts scattered on the floor. And here is the furnace, cold now.

*PNINA SHINEBOURNE*

# Winged

ants crawl out of cracks in the pavement – scurry about in bruised
stones – pause, swirl, reverse, wander along tufts of leaves
huddled in edges. Ants scramble up his easel – a tingling
commotion stirs his eyes – imagine uncle Julius popping out from
under the paving stones, a face uploading a bustle in the high street
– someone is pushing the lid off a manhole, hands rise on a current
of warm air – a rustle, a shiver of hooked-claw legs – an ant takes
off the top of a blade of grass – a mothy-winged Mrs Cole bursts
out of a chest of drawers – swept up on a mating flight – a swarm-
frenzy, launch, flap, spin, soar.
He hears a buzz. He imagines a resurrection.

*PNINA SHINEBOURNE*

# Among

strewn cabbage leaves, bread-crusts too hard
to chew, a double edged comb of a fishbone
and crumpled paper in overflowing dustbins;

amid empty beer bottles and a thicket of rust-
mottled pipes, he found his subject
at the edge of a brushstroke – a glimpse

of heaven in the shape of a cabbage leaf
and a shimmering dot of sunlight crawling
over a teapot cracked at the spout.

*PNINA SHINEBOURNE*

# Capture/Captured

## Capture

the bodies in a grid of pencil lines
against a flower-spattered wallpaper.
Set the point between touching
and cringing, between your legs
stretching out towards her thighs
and her turned-off stare; between
your spectacled pair of eyes
longing to huddle in the folds
of her flesh and her frozen-faced
look, cutting you off
midway between her navel
and her breasts, squashed between
a burning stove and an uncooked
supper, a cold blood-red leg of meat.


## Captured

in a grid of pencil lines lying naked
in crumpled sheets her legs wide apart.
He is squatting between the burning
stove and the uncooked supper,
midway between her navel and her breasts,
legs stretching out towards her thighs;
his bulgy eyes creep into dimples
of flesh, crawl over a crease between
a curve of her shoulder and raised
armpit, skim a cringe at her mouth's edge.
He posed her here but can't make her
touch his hairy chest, this saggy paunch,
nor turn her face towards him, or smile.
Her eyes trace a cold blood-red leg of meat.

*PNINA SHINEBOURNE*

# Resurrection: Kendeja Beach

*(Liberia, 1991)*

Shells by the sea; I shield some in my hand
Still wet with colour, breathless from the game:
*We're winning!* – they gasp and grin – *Against the sand!*
*We beat the pounding! Every day's the same!*
Beware of rough erosion's undertow –
*Not us! We're young and smart. The game is fair.*
*From earth we came, each one. To sand we'll go.*
*We shall be ground, but not today. Not here.*
*We'll dodge the waves. We're lucky, sharp and slight!*
The coast curves on for miles, my hand so small -
*The breakers won't break us. They make us bright!*
Ridiculous, to want to take them all.
The beach is shells; the shells, the beach. No more.
I see some other shells along the shore:

Not shining moons that children hunt with pails,
But dull brown steel that speaks of bodies, piled
Rotting in pools and under palms, like nails,
The mean-mouthed metal shells that hunt the child.
Quite empty now, they'll rust to harmless grain,
Merge with the broken teeth of conch and clam,
While years progress and calm storms come again
To wash away the guilt as best they can;
The blood, the screams, the dreams that walk the shore.
Then sanity might gain some ground at last
And children play across the rocks once more,
Who never held a gun, or took its blast.
But, unaware, with small bare feet, still stand
On broken shells. Too many. Too much sand.

*SARAH SMITH*

# Christmas Stockings, 1936

We woke on the gunmetal brink
to find our black cage cots night-visited
cast off stockings filled to top –
lumps of oranges shaping heels.
We clutched the curved legs to our breasts
gift-thrilled, magic-believers
paused for a moment by dreams fulfilled.
Then a more distant sight intrigued
our rag-knotted heads
a vision not encountered before.
Below us on the floor –
out of reach of striking arms,
beneath the dangling tips of bullet toes
and slumped red jacket soldiers –
row on row of white paper houses,
sudden fragile structures, empty
stables each anticipating its own Christ child.
One girl filled her hand with gleaming marbles,
twisted fires in their hearts,
raised them to her lips
a betrayer's kiss.
As we watched, she stretched
a languid arm out over the paper streets,
parted her fingers,
let those glass bombs fall.

*ANNE SUMMERFIELD*

# Port Glasgow Cemetery, 1947

The Glasgow graves are playing straight here, no
revealing of their solid bodied dead;
no open-arm welcome from relatives,
lovely hope that we have come to expect.
Circled by houses where those buried bided time,
by the sea across which sunsets set, or neighbours drowned,
the graves rest honestly and mostly upright,
sagging here and there to reveal the uneven earth
and the uneven lie of the hill below.
Flowers tell us it is summer, life grows on;
war over, trees remind us, as they branch forth,
where their roots finger quietly.
Perhaps the other pictures that we know
hover and stir this simple one, the presence of
the absent, just beneath the canvas,
tucked between neat paths in their green beds
while the red flowers bloom and suck.
Having been shown in Cookham and elswhere,
limbs do not need to labour, but are sensed.
And yet, the sky is closed and dark ahead.

*ZOË TEALE*

# Christ Overturning
# the Money Changers' Tables

*Stanley Spencer, 1921*

*No!* says the blood-red, blood orange table,
its arms and legs stiff with effort,
*Yes you, in your innocent white shift -*
*leave my moneylenders alone.*
*They're just trying to turn an honest penny,*
*well, as honest as I am.*

*We've been innocent since that great big bang.*
*Where were you when that was going on?*
*The moneylenders and I, we're made of the same stuff,*
*they just came here by a different route.*
*But you? You're made of something different.*

*ROBIN THOMAS*

# Source materials

An old testament, clasped
shut, with snaps inside.
Crispened, pocket
softened, silvering now.
Each one crystallising
a best-remembered place;
Odney Lane and Ricket's
Farm, the Winter Hill in June.
A timed exposure finds
a painter in a churchyard,
one plain, unalterable noon.

*TOM WARD*

# The Betrayal (1922–23)

Past the gate Pa painted last year
Christ appeared. The oak bough shook
drowsily; rooks disbanded, clear
past the gate Pa painted last year.
Saint Peter's bright blade cleaved the ear
of Malchus. Nettles hissed. I looked
past the gate Pa painted last year.
Christ appeared, the oak bough shook.

*TOM WARD*

# The Crucifixion (1958)

I saw him crucified on
Ferry Lane, his light remains
drooped the night long, whereupon
I saw him crucified on
canvas; as soundless and drawn
as any creature in pain.
I saw him crucified on
Ferry Lane. His light remains.

*TOM WARD*

# Disciples

*'The Last Supper', 1920, by Stanley Spencer*

They are fishtails in a box
rowers heaving the boat along

sea birds perched on the gunwale
quietly waiting on His word.

Waves swell beneath the table's deck
Christ at the helm divines his course

John leans to see the hand of God
break bread to cast on the waters.

JEAN WATKINS

# Hilda, Unity and Dolls

*Stanley Spencer, 1937*

Lips are the things you notice first –
the humans' full and sensual like his
dolls' in the rigor of a rosebud smirk.

Next necks – Unity's frail as a mushroom's,
dolls' drainpipe hard. Hilda's rope-like tendons
groan with the stress that's echoed in the set
of her mouth, her inward-looking eyes.

One eye is severed by her spectacles' steel rim,
edge of the picture has trepanned her heavy hair
as though he knew, not knowing, that her apathy
came not from cussedness but illness.

The child whose name had now a bitter taste
stares out, touch of defiance in her lifted chin,
her eyes clear windows. Boredom looks out,
perhaps suppressed dislike, a sense of wrong.

As for the dolls, their masks with black-hole eyes
are sinister, grotesque. Only my fancy, surely,
that their names might be Dorothy and Patricia.

*JEAN WATKINS*

# Sunflower and Dog Worship 1937

Yes, there's great excitement around me
not because I'm trying to turn into a sunflower,

rather the dogs are running loose,
pissing up the wall, playing tongues

with the boy from next door, and my deluded Mrs
is getting fresh with the wrong sunflower,

holding its leaf to her bosom, letting it cradle
her bum, lifting her face to its face.

We're all lusting after... something?
So we change, watched by the curious onlookers,

as we let the chill of fresh air from the currents
of ordinary conversations feed our actions,

and finding memories we've not made,
allow our eyes to wood over.

*JULES WHITING*

# The swans speak to Stanley Spencer

*Separating Fighting Swans*

Don't think we are going to be easy.
Don't be fooled by our whiteness
or the sinuous curve of our necks.

We have a way of disappointing,
of sitting just outside the frame,
reaching in to grab beakfuls of weed.

However, you've made a start.
You've understood we live
in the clash of water, not the stately glide,

that the angels who stand and watch us
have stolen our dimmed feathers
and can only flap uselessly.

You dive for us – small man – try to embrace
a breast, a folded wing
but find that we are muscle

pulsing with hatred. As also with love.
Our nebs' iron clubs, our black forgiving eyes
trapped as you paint us

half twisted to a heart.

*DOROTHY YAMAMOTO*

# Biographies

*MARA ADAMITZ SCRUPE*'s poems have won or been shortlisted for Periplum Book Award, Sentinel Quarterly Book Award, Cornwall Festival Competition, Aesthetica Creative Writing Award, Canterbury Festival/University of Kent Prize, University of Canberra Vice-Chancellor's Award, and National Poetry Society Competition. Her poetry collections include *Sky Pilot* (Finishing Line, 2012) and *BEAST* (NFSPS, 2015).

*VIRGINIA ASTLEY* grew up by the Thames. Her chapbook, *The Curative Harp*, was published in 2015. She is currently completing *Keeping the River*, based on the lives of Thames lock keepers. Last year she won the South Bank prize for *Lost in Locks*. Bloodaxe are publishing her collection in 2018.

*MICHAEL BARTHOLOMEW-BIGGS* is a semi-retired mathematician and poetry editor of the online magazine *London Grip*. Some of his recent ekphrastic poems appear in his latest collection *Pictures from a Postponed Exhibition* (Lapwing Press, 2014) which features the work of Australian artist David Walsh.

*DENISE BENNETT* has an MA in Creative Writing and runs poetry workshops in community settings. Her work has been widely published and she has two collections – *Planting the Snow Queen* and *Parachute Silk* (Oversteps Books) and a pamphlet collection, *Water Chits*, published by Indigo Dreams.

*CAROLE BROMLEY* is a teacher from York. She has two collections with Smith/Doorstop Books, Sheffield, *A Guided Tour of the Ice House* (2012) and *The Stonegate Devil* (2015). A collection of poems for children, *Blast Off!*, will be published in June 2017.

*GRAHAM BURCHELL* lives in South Devon. He has four published collections. He has an MA in Creative Writing from Bath Spa University. He is a Hawthornden Fellow, 2012 Canterbury Festival Poet of the Year, winner of the 2015 Stanza competition, and runner-up in the 2016 BBC Proms poetry competition.

Yorkshire-born former teacher, *LINDA BURNETT* now lives in Nottinghamshire, where she has been writing poetry for the past five years. Still learning her craft, she has won prizes in two Sentinel Annual Competitions, last year's Red Shed postcode prize and has been mentioned in dispatches for several other national competitions.

*JIM CAMPBELL*'s first, and last, collection of poems was published by Fortune Press in 1962, since when there have been several silent decades. He started again two years ago, and has just completed an MA in Creative Writing at Oxford Brookes.

*ROSS COGAN* studied philosophy, gaining a PhD. A writer and editor, he has published two collections, *Stalin's Desk* and *The Book I Never Wrote*, with Oversteps. Ross received a Gregory Award in 1999, and has won the Exeter, Frogmore and Staple prizes, and been placed in others, including the Troubadour. His poetry has been published in various magazines.

Following a professional career in management consultancy, *SHEZ COURTENAY-SMITH* pursued her love of writing as a volunteer with the Stanley Spencer Gallery. As the Gallery's publicist, Shez wrote extensive press material and several magazine features on this great painter. Now a Trustee of the Gallery, Shez was delighted to create a Spencer poem.

*C.L. DALLAT*, poet, musician, critic, (b. Ballycastle, Co. Antrim, lives in London), reviews for *TLS*, *Guardian* and BBC Radio4's *Saturday Review*, won the Strokestown International Poetry Competition, and is The Causley Trust's Causley-centenary poet/musician-in-residence at Charles Causley's house in Cornwall (2017). His latest collection is *The Year of Not Dancing* (Blackstaff). www.cahaldallat.com

*MIRANDA DAY* studied English Literature at Oxford University and Kings College, London and now lives on the edge of Dartmoor. She has worked as a karaoke bar hostess, journalist and English teacher. Her work has appeared in several magazines including *Acumen*, *The Frogmore Papers* and *Dream Catcher*.

*JAN DEAN* is a poet-in-schools and NPD Ambassador for Forward Arts. Her adult poems are in *Double Bill* (Red Squirrel); The *Austen/Bronte/Shakespeare Project* (Like This Press); several *Beautiful Dragons* anthologies and various magazines. From the NW, she lives in the SW and is a Reader in the diocese of Exeter.

*MARGARET DEUTER* was born in Yorkshire but has lived in Bourne End for 26 years. After studying and then teaching languages in Europe and the US, she became a dictionary editor, so words have always played a 'defining' role in her life.

*BRIAN DOCHERTY* was born in Glasgow, lived in London for many years, and now lives on the Sussex coast where he is part of a growing community of writers, artists and musicians. He was educated at Middlesex Polytechnic, University of Essex, London University Institute of Education and St Mary's University College. His books include *Woke Up This Morning* (Smokestack Books, 2012), *Independence Day*, (Penniless Press, 2015), and *In My Dreams, Again* (Penniless Press, 2017).

*ANDY DRAPER* was born in South London in 1951 and his only previously published work was as a runner up in a national children's competition in 1968. Now a retired social worker, his move to Cookham Rise has connected him with a new stimulating environment and a return to creative writing.

*CLAIRE DYER* is a novelist and poet from Reading, Berkshire. Her collections *Interference Effects* and *Eleven Rooms* are published by Two Rivers Press. Her novels are published by Quercus. She has an MA in Creative Writing from Royal Holloway, University of London and her website is www.clairedyer.com.

*JOSH EKROY*'s collection *Ways To Build A Roadblock* is published by Nine Arches Press. He lives in London.

*MICHAEL FITZGERALD* is a writer, contemporary painter and chartered architect who lives in Somerset. He writes poems when he should be doing other things. 'I scribble them down when they come to me, in the middle of meetings or whilst cooking a chicken. Thoughts slip back under if you don't record them.' www.studiofitzgerald.com

*JOHN FOGGIN* lives in West Yorkshire. He has authored four pamphlets, including *Outlaws and Fallen Angels* (Calder valley Poetry 2016). A winner of the Poetry Business International Pamphlet Competition, his first collection *Much Possessed* was published by Smith/Doorstop in 2016. He writes a weekly poetry blog: http://johnfoggin.wordpress. com.

*JOHN GALLAS* is a New Zealand poet. He has 16 books published, mostly by Carcanet (10) and Cold Hub NZ (3). He is a Fellow of the English Association and a St Magnus Orkney Festival poet. His new book, *The Little Sublime Comedy* from Carcanet is due this July. He has just completed John Clare's walk from Epping Forest to Northborough, *Mad John's Walk*, published by Five Leaves (Nottingham).

*CAROLINE GILL* was Overall Winner in the Zoological Society of London Poetry Competition (2014). Her chapbook, *The Holy Place*, was co-authored with John Dotson and published by The Seventh Quarry (Wales, 2012) with Cross-Cultural Communications (New York). Caroline's poem, 'Elegy for Idris Davies', received a 2014 Pushcart nomination. www.carolinegillpoetry.com

*HELENA GODDARD* has been writing poetry for ten years and has been placed or commended in various competitions during that time. In 2016 she came third in the Plough Poetry Competition, was commended in the Interpreter's House competition, and appeared on the shortlist of the Bridport.

*JACEY GOMME* was born in Amersham and grew up thereabouts, his forebears including Thomas Robinson, designer of Reading's Attwells Fountain, and Sydney Gomme, Watford architect. He started wandering in the 1970s, and has been variously employed, early on with auctioneers in Amersham, homeless in Bedford and hospitalized in Cambridge.

*GILES GOODLAND* has published several books of poetry including *A Spy in the House of Years* (2001), *Capital* (2006), *What the Things Sang* (2009) and *The Dumb Messengers* (2012). A new book from Shearsman is due soon. He works in Oxford as a lexicographer and lives in West London.

*MARYLOU GRIMBERG* lived in Singapore for 17 years, and her five children were born there. She now has 10 grandchildren. Before the children left home the family had horses, dogs and cats in profusion. Once they were grown Marylou went back to school and received a PhD in Linguistics from UCL.

*EMMA HARDING*'s poems have been published in a number of magazines and anthologies including *Poetry Review*, *Stand*, *Magma* and *The North*.

*HILARY HARES* has an MA in Poetry from Manchester Metropolitan University. Her poems have found homes in fifty magazines and anthologies including *Ink*, *Sweat and Tears*, *The Interpreter's House*, *Obsessed with Pipework*, *South* and *Under the Radar*. She is currently putting finishing touches to her first collection, *Re-inventing the Red Queen*.

*MARK HAWORTH-BOOTH* worked as a curator at the Victoria and Albert Museum, 1970–2004, and wrote standard works on the history of photography and design. His poems have appeared in national magazines since 1987 and he published *Wild Track: Poems with Pictures by Friends* in 2005. He lives in North Devon.

*MAEVE HENRY* lives in Oxford, and is married with three children. She works for the NHS and is currently completing a Masters in Creative Writing at Oxford Brookes. Her poems were shortlisted for the Flambard Poetry Prize in 2016, and longlisted for the National Poetry Competition in 2015.

*KAREN IZOD*: consultant to social and cultural change, academic writer, creative writer: attachment, birds, wild places, thin places, city spaces, people, politics. Published: *Agenda* (Dempsey & Windle), *Attachment* (Paper Swans). Online: Karnacology, New Welsh Review video-showcase, Poetry Shed, Zoomorphic. Spoken word: Write out Loud Woking, 1000 Monkeys Guildford. karenizod@virginmedia.com

*ROSIE JACKSON* lives in Somerset and teaches creative writing. Her poetry is widely published, including *What the Ground Holds* (Poetry Salzburg, 2014), *The Light Box* (Cultured Llama, 2016), and journals. She's taught at East Anglia and other universities. Her memoir *The Glass Mother* (Unthank Books) came out in 2016. www.rosiejackson.org.uk

*PAUL JEFFCUTT* has won prizes for poetry in England, Scotland, Ireland and the USA. His debut collection, *Latch*, published by Lagan Press in 2010, was chosen by *The Ulster Tatler* as their Book of the Month. He co-hosts The Squat Pen, a series of literary events that take place across the island of Ireland. www.pauljeffcutt.net

*HELEN KIDD*'s collection *Blue Weather* won the Cork Manuscript Competition in 2004. She recently contributed to several anthologies, including *Poems for Jeremy Corbyn*, *The Wild Atlantic Way*, *Zoomorphic*, and *The Deep Heart's Core*. She was co-editor of the *Virago Book of Love Poetry* and contributed to many books on poetry. Sadly, she died in April 2017 (see p.xx).

*GILL LEARNER* lives in Reading and loves walking along the Thames near Cookham. She has won several prizes, including the Poetry Society's Hamish Canham award, and been published in many magazines and anthologies. Her collections, *The Agister's Experiment* (2011) and *Chill Factor* (2016), are from Two Rivers Press. http://www.poetrypf.co.uk/gilllearnerpage.shtml

*JOHN LOVEDAY* will be 91 in April 2017. He loves oil painting and has retired from a career in education. His novel *Halo* won McKitterick & David Higham prizes in 1992 and *Goodbye, Buffalo Sky*, Best Children's Book Award in 1994. His selected poems, *Particular Sunlights*, was published in 1983. His new child's-eye account of 1930s Norfolk life is awaiting a publisher.

*TONY LUCAS*, though christened and married in Cookham church, has lived all his adult life in London. His poetry has been published in America as well the UK. A new collection of his work, *Unsettled Accounts*, was brought out by Stairwell Books last winter.

*CHRISTINE MACFARLANE* was born in Liverpool and spent part of her childhood in Malaysia. Having worked as a teacher, primary headteacher and lecturer, she now writes full time. Her work has been longlisted for Bridport 2016 and National Poetry Competition 2014; 'A letter to William Shakespeare' has been accepted for publication in *Poetry Salzburg*. She lives in Somerset with her husband; they have four children.

*LORRAINE MARINER* has published two collections with Picador, *Furniture* (2009) and *There Will Be No More Nonsense* (2014). She has been shortlisted for the Forward Prize twice for Best Single Poem and Best First Collection and for the Seamus Heaney Centre Poetry Prize.

*ALWYN MARRIAGE*'s ten books include poetry collections, non-fiction and, most recently, a novel, *Rapeseed*; and she's widely represented in magazines, anthologies and online. Formerly a university philosophy lecturer, Director of two international NGOs and a Rockefeller Scholar, she's currently Managing Editor of Oversteps Books and research fellow at Surrey University. www.marriages.me.uk/alwyn.

*STEPHEN JAMES MOORE* studied in Newcastle and Brighton and now lives and writes in Bristol. He is working on a full poetry collection concerning heart health, a documentary poetry film about a lost poet and a play called *Porcelain*. He works at a specialized cardiac catheterization suite. He enjoys running, photography and art.

*JILL MUNRO*'s first collection *Man from La Paz* was published in 2015 by Green Bottle Press. She won the Fair Acre Press Pamphlet Competition 2015 with *The Quilted Multiverse*, published 2016. She has been longlisted three times for the National Poetry Competition. Jill lives and works in Crowborough, East Sussex.

*KATE NOAKES'* sixth collection is *Paris, Stage Left* (Eyewear, 2017). She is a Welsh Academician and her website (boomslangpoetry. blogspot.com) is archived by the National Library of Wales. She lives and writes in London and Paris.

*PATRICK B. OSADA* is an editor, writes reviews of poetry for magazines and is a member of the Management Team for *SOUTH Poetry Magazine*. His first collection, *Close to the Edge*, was published in 1996 and won the prestigious Rosemary Arthur Award. He has published four collections, with a fifth, *Changes*, published in January 2017. Patrick's work has been widely published in magazines, anthologies and on the internet. For more information about his work and a selection of his poetry, visit www.poetry-patrickosada.co.uk.

*TOM PHILLIPS* is a poet, playwright and translator whose work has been published in a wide variety of journals, anthologies, pamphlets and the full-length collections *Recreation Ground* (Two Rivers Press, 2012) and *Unknown Translations* (Scalino, 2016). He is the co-founder of the online art/poetry project Colourful Star and the editor of Balkan Poetry Today.

*CHARLIE PLEDGER* is an award-winning photojournalist. He started writing poetry in response to his work covering the wars in Afghanistan and Iraq. Much of his poetry complements his photo essays detailing the small moments of experience that can't be fully conveyed in a photograph.

*IAN POPLE*'s *Saving Spaces* is published by Arc.

*VICTORIA PUGH* lives in Reading and teaches at Reading College. She has an MA in Creative Writing from Manchester Metropolitan University. Her first collection, *Mrs Marvellous*, was published by Two Rivers Press in 2008. One of her poems was highly commended and published in The Forward Book of Poetry 2009.

*RICHARD ROBBINS* was raised in California and Montana but has lived continuously in Minnesota since 1984. His *Body Turn to Rain: New and Selected Poems* is due from Lynx House Press in May 2017. He currently directs the creative writing programme at Minnesota State Mankato.

*KIM ROONEY* writes poetry and short fiction. She was first published by *Spare Rib* in 1978. Her poem, 'At the end', won second prize in the 2007 English Association Fellows' Poetry Prize. Kim has an MA in Life Writing from the University of East Anglia. She lives in Lancashire.

*LESLEY SAUNDERS* is an award-winning author of several books and pamphlets of poetry, published mostly by Two Rivers Press. Lesley runs writing workshops for public organizations and local groups, and has held several interesting residencies. She undertakes editorial and mentoring work as well as book reviewing. More details at www.lesleysaunders.org.uk.

*ROBERT SAXTON*, born in Nottingham in 1952, lives in north London. He is the author of six books of poetry: from Enitharmon, *The Promise Clinic*; from Carcanet/Oxford*Poets*, *Manganese*, *Local Honey* and *Hesiod's Calendar*; from Shearsman, *The China Shop Pictures*; and from Angle Shades Press, *Six-way Mirror*. www.robertsaxton.co.uk.

*PNINA SHINEBOURNE* was born and grew up in Israel. Her pamphlet, *A Suburb of Heaven*, won the 2014 Venture/flipped eye poetry pamphlet award. Her first collection is forthcoming in 2017 with Smokestack books. She teaches psychology at Middlesex University and lives in London.

*SARAH SMITH* writes poetry for page and stage. She regularly reads at the Dreading Poetry Slam in Reading, winning their Slam Masters Tournament in 2016. Her day job is Head of Communications for an international charity, before which she had a 10-year stint in academia, teaching Economic, Social and Cultural History.

*ANNE SUMMERFIELD* has loved Spencer's painting for many years and used to visit the Spencer Gallery often. She writes poetry and fiction and is published in the 2017 Aesthetica Writing Annual as well as in magazines including *Mslexia*, *Orbis*, and *The Interpreter's House*. She tweets infrequently as @summerwriter.

*ZOË TEALE* read English at St Catherine's College, Oxford, and Social Anthropology at The London School of Economics. Her novel, *Sir Phoebus' Ma*, was published by Orion, and she has had poems and short stories published in a few anthologies. She lives in Oxford.

*ROBIN THOMAS* has had poems accepted by *Agenda, Envoi, Orbis, Brittle Star, Pennine Platform, The High Window* and *Poetry Scotland* among others. His pamphlet *A Fury of Yellow* was published by Eyewear in November 2016. A collection of his poetry will be published by Cinnamon Press in early 2018.

*TOM WARD* is a Scottish poet based in London, where he works as an Art Technician. He is interested in objects and what they reveal about the way we live. He can be found online @artinconnu.

*JEAN WATKINS'* poems have appeared in many anthologies and magazines. Her first collection, *Scrimshaw*, was published by Two Rivers Press in 2013, and her second, *Precarious Lives*, is forthcoming from the same publisher in 2018.

*JULES WHITING* grew up in Cholsey, Oxfordshire. She received an MA in Creative Writing from Bath Spa University. Her poems have appeared in *Orbis, South, Envoi, The Interpreters House* and various anthologies. She was short listed for the Plough prize 2016.

*DOROTHY YAMAMOTO* lives in Oxford and writes non-fiction books about animals, as well as poetry.

Two Rivers Press has been publishing in and about Reading since 1994. Founded by the artist Peter Hay (1951–2003), the press continues to delight readers, local and further afield, with its varied list of individually designed, thought-provoking books.